Parties For All Occasions

BARNES LARGE TYPE EDITIONS

Amateur Cabinetmaking, by Vernon M. Albers
Amateur Furniture Construction, by Vernon M. Albers
The Book of Country Crafts, by Randolph Wardell Johnston
Chess in Ten Lessons, by Larry Evans
Creative Cooking without Wheat, Milk and Eggs, by Ruth R. Shattuck
How To Fish in Salt Water, by Vlad Evanoff
How to Grow Food for Your Family, by Samuel R. Ogden
How to Use Woodworking Tools Effectively and Safely, by Vernon M. Albers
Parties for All Occasions, by Carlson Wade
Pocket Billiards with Cue Tips, by Edward D. Knuchell
Pull Up an Easel, Revised Edition, by Norman Garbo
The Repair and Reupholstering of Old Furniture, by Vernon M. Albers
The Science of Checkers and Draughts, by Tom Wiswell
You Can Play Par Golf, by Charles Bassler and Nevin H. Gibson

By the Same Author:

THE COMPLETE RICE COOKBOOK

Parties for All Occasions

CARLSON WADE

Illustrations by Elsie Hanauer

South Brunswick and New York: A. S. Barnes and Company
London: Thomas Yoseloff Ltd

Library of Congress Catalogue Card Number: 76-37819

A. S. Barnes and Co., Inc.
Cranbury, New Jersey 08512

Thomas Yoseloff Ltd
108 New Bond Street
London W1Y OQX, England

First Printing of Large Type Edition 1976

ISBN 0-498-01882-2 (Large Type Edition)
Printed in the United States of America

Dedicated to

CHARLES CHINTALA

who made it all possible

Contents

Introduction

You can enjoy a successful shower party! This book was written to take the confusion and fears out of planning, holding and attending a joyful shower party—either as a guest, a hostess or the special guest of honor. This book was written to guide you from the start to the happy finish of a shower party whether it be to fete a bride-to-be or an approaching baby, an anniversary, a housewarming, an office party—you name it! This book is the outgrowth of endless research with experts in the field, and the accumulation of practical experience in enjoying successful shower parties. Now, all of this easy-to-follow etiquette, suggestions, ideas, advice is presented to you in one handy volume.

A Shower Is a Special Kind of a Party

When you're planning a shower, it simply isn't enough to say, "Come over on Thursday and bring a gift for Alice," and then forget until Thursday about the event. When you're planning an ordinary party, it's easy to round up a few guests who bring themselves, a friendly smile and little in the way of obligations. But a *shower* is a special kind of party that is given for someone else and etiquette prevails because it calls for gift-giving amongst friends. This makes it unique and something that has to be planned and properly programmed in order to strengthen the friendship, rather than run the risk of spoiling the friendship.

A Shower Is Easy and Fun-Filled

As you will see, a shower is one of the easiest forms of entertainment. Its very simplicity suggests caution—it should not be underdone or overdone. With the properly measured "ingredients," a shower can be a festive occasion that will be enjoyed and long remembered by all who participate.

Plan Your Shower for Happy Success

This book will show you how to plan your shower for happy success—*the easy way!* A basic rule here is to plan everything (from guest list to actual party) with the *theme* in mind. If you use this basic rule in planning your shower, then you should have a memorable success. *Special Note:* Because a shower is a direct bid for gifts, such a party was long frowned upon in conservative circles. For this reason, proper planning is essential so it will become a happy, joyous party, rather than a "gift giving" obligation. Today, shower parties are becoming more and more popular for a wide range of affairs from bridal occasions to a housewarming or just for having a good time. Always keep in mind that the *theme* determines the arrangement of the shower—and that gift giving should be done with mutual approval and happiness.

Showers: More Fun Than Parties

With proper planning, as outlined in this volume, showers can become more fun than ordinary parties. They could even be more popular than parties and make you a coveted hostess. So . . . plan your way to shower success and have fun!

1.
The Etiquette of Successful Shower Parties

Because there are social authorities who consider shower parties an excuse for gift-giving, it is wise to observe certain rules of etiquette so that you will not offend others or be offended yourself. Surely, shower parties provide enjoyment, express a feeling of friendship and love, and help promote social status in your circle. Shower parties also help make participants more welcome in the community and in their social set. Plus—shower parties are fun!

Should You Give the Shower?

One etiquette rule that is seldom broken is that the person (or the families of the person or persons) to be honored, does *not* call for or give the shower. Because a shower party calls for a gift, it is improper for a bride-to-be or an anniversary celebrating couple to give the shower. In effect, it is the same as saying, "We're holding a party. You're invited and bring a gift."

Instead, close friends of the guest of honor get together, decide that there will be a shower and make all the necessary arrangements. *Exception:* In the case of a housewarming, or a family celebration with only relatives participating, the guest-of-honor may give the party. A housewarming calls for bringing gifts to the person who has just moved into a new house or apartment. Since shower parties are usually surprise affairs, it would be unwise to spring a "Surprise" on the occupants who might be fast asleep or otherwise indisposed when you come knocking at the door. So, a housewarming is usually planned with the occupant-guest of honor knowing when it will take place in his house. A close relative shower party "for the family only" means that a relative may plan the affair. Other than these exceptions, it is improper for either the guest-of-honor or members of the family to call for a shower.

Basic Rule: A close friend of the guest of honor decides to give the shower; she speaks with other close friends and the arrangements are made.

Where to Hold a Shower?

Usually, a shower party is a surprise event. It is done without the foreknowledge of the guest of honor, although she may secretly suspect its arrangement when friends ask her if she has nothing to do next Saturday and would she want to join them for tea at someone else's house. So, to keep the surprise as part of the good fun of a shower party, it should be held at the home of the close friend who suggested it in the first place.

The home where the shower is to be held is the source from which invitations are mailed. The person who holds the shower in her home is known as the *hostess.* The friends who attend the shower are known as *guests.* The person being feted is the *guest of honor.* Accordingly, you conduct yourself in that proper manner—being a friendly hostess, a respectful guest, a worthy guest-of-honor.

Informality Is The Key. Except on certain occasions, informality is the key to a successful and fun-filled shower party. Be casual, but be careful not to offend others. You are all friends and should be cordial toward one another—behaving as friends. Keep it informal and have fun—but keep it respectful, too.

What Are the Socially Accetable Purposes for a Shower?

Any event that calls for the bringing of a gift is acceptable for a shower. The most popular purposes are a bride-to-be shower and a baby shower. But with more leisure time among us, showers are being used to celebrate anniversaries, the changing of the seasons, a new promotion, office celebration, birthdays, legal holidays, religious holidays, special occasions such as having won an award, as well as knowing what a guest of honor needs and wanting to fill that need.

Example: You know a nice young couple who is struggling to make ends meet. You visited them one evening, and noted a scarcity of linens. You want to offer a helping hand, but feel you will offend or embarrass them by bringing them some linens. It may look like charity! So, you call up a few close friends, have an understanding and arrange a shower party at *your* home. All of the close friends bring different types of linen for the young couple. A *linen shower* is a fun-filled party that the young couple will like and will not feel they are the recipients of charity. *Note:* the theme of the shower should ALWAYS be in keeping with the needs of the guest of honor. In this situation, the young couple needed linens and were thus feted.

Suggestion: You visited the home of a good friend, noted that there was an absence of cheerful floral decorations in her modest surroundings. You do not want to suggest that she brighten up with flowers since you may offend her. What to do? Wait until the first day of Spring. On that day, surprise the friend with a shower party in which you and other close friends bring potted plants or live flowers, and inexpensive artificial flowers arranged in wreaths, in vases, or in groups. You have fulfilled a need and kept within the realm of good taste, because flowers are always associated with early Spring.

Keep in mind the personal needs of the guest of honor, work it in with a related theme, and you should have a happy shower party.

What Kind of Shower to Give?

Anticipate the needs of the guest of honor and then create a shower to fit those particuplar needs. The gifts reflect the needs of the guest of honor. *Tip:* Because a shower is *informal,* it does not call for elaborate arrangements. Often, a simple tea-and-cookies arrangement will suffice. A buffet luncheon is the most popular. Or, a dinner-in-a-dish for the evening. But keep it simple. The same applies to the type of shower.

Example: A young member of the family is starting college. His family provides for most of his needs, but his friends want to show an amicable spirit and well-wishing toward this freshman student. So they secretly plan to surprise him with a shower party at someone's home. They give him a "Homework Kit" Shower. They give him an assortment of writing materials, notebooks, small pocket dictionaries, a little globe, even small books that will help him in his studies. An inexpensive loose-leaf book with ample supplies of paper is always welcome. Here we see that the shower theme, starting in college, is consistent with the gifts that are given.

When Should You Hold a Shower?

The most popular time for a shower is in the early afternoon or luncheon time. However, the rules are flexible. Here is a brief list of three times during the day to hold a shower and how to observe successful etiquette standards:

1. BREAKFAST TIME SHOWER.

Your table should be kept simple. Serve breakfast to the guests. You might begin serving fresh fruit, then a hot dish, rolls and lots of piping hot coffee. Present gifts to the guest of honor *after* the breakfast.

2. LUNCHEON TIME SHOWER.

For this type of shower, the guests are usually women, married or single. Serve luncheon to the guests. You could begin with soup, salad or a fruit cocktail as the first course; follow with a casserole dish and then with dessert and a beverage. If you have a large group and cannot accommodate them around your dining table, try serving them on card tables covered with gaily printed luncheon cloths. *Suggestion:* In nice weather, try having a luncheon time shower on the porch or on your lawn, if you have one.

3. EVENING TIME SHOWER.

This type of shower is one that calls for men as guests. Since most men have to work during the day, it would be wise to have a dinner shower when they're invited. Serve dinner to your guests. Have soup or a fruit cocktail as a starter; then have a main dish such as a casserole that is easy to prepare and eat; then serve cakes or pastries with a hot beverage for dessert.

Suggestions:

Because shower parties may take too much time, it is increasingly popular to hold them in the evening—after all the guests, themselves, have eaten at home. This means that the guests arrive at the hostess' home, bring gifts, greet the guest-of-honor, and have a lot of fun together without the need for a time-consuming meal. It is wise to serve simple cakes or sandwiches with ices, punch, or tea as the only refreshments.

Whom to Invite to the Shower?

Again, keep in mind that a shower calls for gift-giving, so invite *only* close friends who personally know the guest-of-honor. It would be an imposition to invite casual acquaintances, or to tell the guests to bring along their own friends who may not even know the guest of honor. Yet, everyone is obligated to bring a gift, and it is offensive to expect a stranger to do so—just as it is offensive to expect the guest-of-honor to take a gift from a perfect stranger whom she may never again see! So the simple etiquette rule is to invite only close friends.

Should Men Be Invited to Showers?

By all means! It is unfortunate that showers were formerly all-female affairs; even today, men are rarely invited to a shower—although many men become guests-of-honor, depending upon the theme. So many showers are given for the bride-to-be, that it seems unfair to neglect the groom-to-be. Without him, there would be no marriage!

Suggestion: The hostess should make careful planning for a shower that may include men. If the shower party calls for the giving of intimate lingerie or delicate "for women only" items, then it would be best to eliminate the men. By careful planning, you can make a shower a fun-filled party, rather than an embarrassed red-faced experience.

If a shower is held to give gifts to a young housewife or to help fill up one room of the house such as the kitchen, or if a shower is held to welcome a new clergyman to help furnish the rectory or his study, it is wise to include men.

We emphasize again—keep within the *theme* of the shower and the types of gifts that are given and then decide if the male members of the group would fit in.

Should You Have a Time Schedule?

By all means! Without a time schedule, your shower party could become an unhappy affair that spells embarrassment and lost friendship. Here is a brief at-a-glance schedule to help you plan your shower:

1. Get together with several friends and decide *who* is to be showered. Decide upon the purpose for the gift giving which can range from a wedding-to-be to a Halloween party.
2. Select the home where the shower will be held. Plan in advance to have everything available on that specific date.
3. Sound out the guest of honor and discreetly ask if she will be free on that specific time and date. Say you are holding an informal tea party and that she "just must come or else everyone will be disappointed." *Remember:* much of the fun of a shower party is in the surprise. Get a definite okay before you proceed.
4. Send out your invitations at least two weeks to one month *before* the shower date. *Note:* The home or apartment in which the shower will be held means that the resident becomes the hostess. She is the one who has to prepare the invitations, mail them out, receive telephone acknowledgments,

take care of cancellations and other details. Of course, friends help the hostess as much as possible, but she does have the responsibility of preparing everything. She is, after all, the hostess!

5. Decide how long the shower will last. It is best to set a time limit of about *two hours.* This gives the guests and the guest of honor enough time to share appreciation of the gifts and to partake of refreshments, with lots of friendly chatting. *Note:* If you extend the shower for a prolonged time, you may wear out the guest of honor and also wear out your own welcome! Most guests of honor have other things to do, such as preparing for a wedding, blessed event, special affair, so they should be given the courtesy of a two-hour time limit to the shower. Announce the time limit, gently, in advance.

6. Gently decline any offers of friends who wish to stay behind and help tidy up. Above all, refuse the guest of honor's offer of help since it is imprudent to have her do the cleaning up at a shower party in her honor! It would be best to do it all by yourself and avoid the embarrassment of obligations. You have opened your home or apartment for your guests and you should not create an ill feeling by having others help you in the cleaning up—no matter how strongly they insist. A little extra elbow grease on your part in tidying up alone, will go a long way to keep your friendship lubricated!

Enjoy a Fun-Filled Shower Party.

While gift-giving for a special theme is the reason for holding a shower, its benefit is to provide lots of happy and healthy fun for all participants. It is joyful to help others furnish a household, welcome the baby, or celebrate a local event or affair. It is a good feeling to help others with a shower party —as you would want them to help you, too! Observe the etiquette rules and enjoy a fun-filled shower party.

2.

Shower Invitations: How to Invite Guests

Because shower parties automatically call for gift-giving, the guests should be carefully selected. As already stated, the shower is basically made by close and intimate friends of the guest of honor. Strangers seem out of place—especially when they are obligated to give gifts. So, the initial rule is to invite only those who know the guest of honor—and who know her personally. Stick to this rule, and you will have a good chance of success.

When To Invite Members of the Family.

If the shower occasion is that of an anniversary, a house-warming, a bon voyage, or any celebration that is a *family affair,* then members of the immediate family most certainly belong at the event.

Otherwise, it is best to include solely friends of the guest of honor.

Use Tact and Common Sense with Guest List Selection.

Let's face it—many "friends" do not seem to get along

with each other at parties or in close confinement. Two office co-workers may get along well when they're side by side at their desks—but they bicker and quarrel when they're at lunch or out on a special affair. If this is the case, you would do well to keep such persons away from the shower or invite just one of them. *Note:* it is often said that while some personalities click perfectly, others may clash. *Example:* Lillian W. chatters incessantly. Andrew E. likes peace and quiet. So, invite either one or neither of them, since they may get on one another's nerves when put closely together at a shower party. *Example:* Rita E. is a chain-smoker and casual friend Mary T. has an aversion to smokers. Either invite one of them, neither of them, or very gently suggest that Rita try to smoke elsewhere to avoid being offensive.

A bit of careful planning will help you prepare a good guest list of personalities and friends who will have fun, and not find fault with or complain about one another.

Do Not Use a Shower Party to Bring Divided Friends Together.

There are times when you feel like playing the Girl Scout and want to bring two divided friends together. A shower is *not* the place to do it. If you force two estranged people together at a social affair, you risk disaster. This is a wrong combination and is as ailing as a wrong food combination. *Also:* try to separate those who have strongly determined contrary views about politics, race, religion, business, or even marriage itself. All it takes is one wrong word to start an argument and the shower can turn into a wet blanket!

Select Guests Who Want to Come to the Shower.

You will have a rousing success if you will select only those guests who are personally interested in the theme and the guest of honor. To invite someone who is disinterested, or who is being "forced" to attend because you feel she should be there, is improper and unnecessary. No one can have fun at a shower if she did not want to come in the first place. *Never* obligate someone by saying she must attend a shower party. *Always* invite those guests who genuinely want to come.

Remember: it cannot be repeated too often that a shower calls for gift-giving and it is an imposition as well as an embarrassment to have a casual or unwelcome guest grudgingly offer a gift to the guest of honor.

Note: a shower is *not* the proper occasion for the repayment of a social obligation or the introduction of a new friend to your group. Keep match-making out of shower parties! It is a slight to the guest of honor!

How to Send Your Invitations.

Once you have selected your list of names and addresses of close friends, you have to formally send them printed invitations notifying them of the time and place of the shower.

(*Note:* It is best to send a printed invitation since this helps each person remember the date. A telephone invitation may be used *only* if the shower is a tiny one, with less than 5 or 6 guests. Even then, a written invitation would be advisable.)

Hostess Sends Invitations.

The selected hostess, at whose home the shower party will take place, is responsible for sending the invitations. You should mail them in time so guests can make necessary preparations; they have to select, purchase and wrap gifts. They have to reserve the time and evening. A wise suggestion is for you to mail invitations, by first class mail, from two to four weeks before the agreed-upon date. This helps everyone make proper plans.

USE CUTE INVITATIONS.

Emphasize the *theme* in your written invitation. Many five-and-ten stores as well as party goods shops have special invitations for various occasions. You just sign your name and fill in the other necessary information. But you may want to make your own invitations. This means you reflect the mood and atmosphere of the shower theme.

Examples: A bride-to-be shower calls for wedding garment drawings, cute sketches or illustrations. A stork shower calls for pink and/or blue cards with cute little sketches. A kitchen shower calls for pots and pans and other paraphernalia sketched on the invitations. You may use verse, a bit of decoration, novelty notepaper—as well as any of the suggestions given in the following chapter, for each specific theme.

WRITE IT FIRST—SAY IT SECOND.

A written invitation gives the guest time to consult her calendar to decide definitely if she will attend. It is also more likely to be accurately understood when all the information is written down. To confirm, telephone your listed guests a few days before the date. When telephoning guests, speak directly to them. Messages left with others may be forgotten and cause misunderstandings among otherwise good friends.

Select Appropriate Age Groups.

There should be no age limit to consider when inviting shower guests. Any person who is familiar and close to the guest of honor should be included. There may be some ex-

MISCELLANEOUS SHOWER INVITATIONS

Cut invitations from colorful construction paper. Draw in details with colored felt tip pens.

SHOWER INVITATIONS

Bride-to-be Invitation

Stork Shower Invitation

Kitchen Shower Invitation

ceptions that call for the hostess' discretion. *Example:* A teen-age girl might feel uncomfortable in the "generation gap" if her shower includes over-40 guests. At this sensitive age, it might be wise to include only those to whom she can relate in her adolescent years. *Example:* A couple celebrating their 50th anniversary might feel strange if they have long-haired guitar players at their shower, even if they are known to them. In this situation, it would be best to invite only those guests who have similar age interests.

Invite a Guest—Not a Gift.

The guests will all know the basic *theme* of the party and this tells them what types of gifts to give. But you do *not* tell the guests exactly what to bring, or how much (or how little) to spend. This is not in good taste. Each guest has her own personal budget and she will want to use personal judgment in selecting an appropriate gift that may have a delicate significance. The best plan is to let each guest decide for herself without any suggestions on your part . . . except when asked for advice. In that event, be cordial and let the guest make up her own mind with a little help from yourself. Invite a guest—not a gift!

Six Items to Be Included on Your Invitation.

No matter how the invitations are made, they should be clearly specific, listing the following six items:

1. Full name of the guest of honor.
2. The exact time for the invited guest to arrive.
3. The month, day and year of the shower party.
4. The exact address where the shower party will be held.
5. Describe the specific type of shower and the theme.

6. Give the name of the hostess, her telephone number.

TIP: At the bottom of the invitation, include R.S.V.P. which means that each invited guest can telephone you to confirm the invitation. Keep a check list of those who call you. Any who fail to do so should be telephoned. Perhaps the missive was lost in the mail. This takes a few moments, and provides much success!

How to Invite the Guest of Honor to the Surprise Shower.

It is a good idea to get the guest of honor's definite acceptance to appear at this "gathering" before you make any plans. Since this will be a surprise, you simply ask her if she can come to the gathering, the "tea party," the "party" on that given date. Be firm about her commitment. Say that you will reserve a table for her and that she must come. It is disastrous to hold a shower party at which the guest of honor just doesn't show up! *Tip:* When she agrees to come to the appointed place, take out a notepad and mark it down while she is watching. This exerts a friendly obligation on her part to attend. Telephone her a day before to confirm it.

Tell the Guest of Honor It Is to Be a Party.

No person would feel happy at suddenly being thrust in the center of attraction, after spending a frazzling day doing housework or office work. Your guest of honor should know this is to be a party and she should prepare herself accordingly for it. Of course, she is not told it is to be a shower, only that it is a social gathering and to look her nicest. This will help avoid any misunderstandings.

Invite Congenial Guests for a Jolly Affair.

Your shower party will be a jolly affair if your guests are selected with care. They should be warm, friendly guests, congenial toward one another. See that they have common interests, that they are all friends, that they *want* to give gifts to show their appreciation of their friendship; and see that the guest of honor is worthy of being so celebrated.

Often, the key to a successful shower party lies in a careful selection of invited guests. When you can gather a happy assortment of good friends together, who come bearing welcomed gifts, you have the makings of a successful shower party.

3.

So You're Invited to a Shower

A Shower Is a Gift Is a Shower!

When you accept an invitation to a shower, you automatically agree to bring a gift. It need not be expensive, but should be something rather useful and in keeping with the theme and purpose of the shower. Here are the accepted rules and etiquette tips that will help put fun and success into the gift-giving and gift-receiving of the shower party.

Include Your Name and Good Wishes with Your Gift.

Each gift, whether sent or taken, should be accompanied with a card bearing your name and address and good wishes for the guest of honor. This will enable your guest of honor to thank you, personally, for your gift.

Gifts Should Be Presented in Person.

Each invited guest should present her gift in person. It is considered poor taste to send a gift, except in situations of extreme dire hardship, or illness. If you cannot attend the shower party for any other reason, then it would be best to decline the invitation at the time when it is made and just not send any gift at all. To send in a gift without an appearance gives the impression that you were forced into it and fulfilled your "obligation" by giving a gift but you need not make a personal appearance. Because the shower party is a friendly one, it is wise to make an appearance with a gift, or just be completely absent (gift and all) if you have reasons other than personal hardship for abstaining.

Tips on Bringing a Proper Gift.

Part of planning calls for anticipating the needs of the guest of honor as well as the theme of the shower. In the following chapters, we offer you specific ideas for specific occasions. But there are some general rules and tips that will make you a welcome guest and gift-bringer:

1. Keep the needs and tastes of the guest of honor in mind when selecting the gift. *Example:* If she is a serious businesswoman type, select useful, practical gifts. She may not care for frilly garments or colorful hats.

2. If in doubt about size, avoid clothing gifts. Size is often vital for a personal type of shower. The guest of honor may be asked discreetly about her size. Otherwise, ask her mother, or a close member of the family so you can purchase the correct size of a clothing gift. If you are still in doubt, then settle for a non-wearing gift.

3. Try to learn the color schemes in advance. If the gifts are to be used in the guest of honor's household, try to learn the color schemes in advance to avoid possible clashes. *Example:* Dozens of pink towels and wash cloths as well as a pink bath mat would go well with a blue bathroom. But . . . what if it is an ivory bathroom and the colors clash? Take a little time to find out if your gift colors will blend in with the

decor. *Also:* You have just knitted a lovely blue sweater that is the exact size of the honoree; then you learn that she hates the color blue. Again, a few casual words to inquire of a favorite color will do much to help make you a welcome shower guest.

4. Have all gifts gaily wrapped, to harmonize with the decorations and the theme. Many five-and-ten stores and special party shops have appropriate wrapping paper.

5. All gifts may either be brought when you arrive, or sent ahead so the hostess can arrange them properly and have everything in order for the shower party.

Where to Put the Gifts as You Begin the Shower.

The hostess takes all the gifts and places them either on a table or behind a screen, or in a special room that is kept closed to the guest of honor until the "surprise" moment.

Two types of receptacles seem to be most popular:

1. *Wishing Well.* Use a very large waste paper basket covered with crepe paper in a stone or brick pattern. Or, have a wooden frame about thirty inches high by thirty-six inches wide and covered with patterned paper. As guests arrive, the gifts are placed in the Wishing Well or behind the frame. When all are assembled, then the guest of honor may start drawing gifts from the "well."

2. *Umbrella.* Take a standard umbrella and open it fully. Cover it (round and round) with gaily colored crepe paper or with white paper streamers and with a huge paper bow on the handle. Gifts are piled under the umbrella. When all are assembled, then the guest of honor may start drawing gifts from the "good luck umbrella."

THE WISHING WELL

This Wishing Well is easily made from a box, wood strips, wood-grained wallpaper, brick pattern crepe paper, glue and a few tacks.

Follow the simple steps shown below.

Cut wood strips pointed.

Glue the wood strips to the inside of the box. Then tack from the outside.

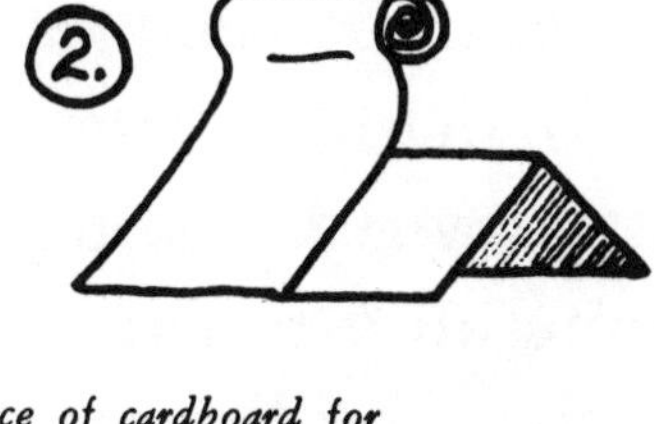

Fold a piece of cardboard for the roof and cover with wallpaper. Also cover the box with brick pattern paper.

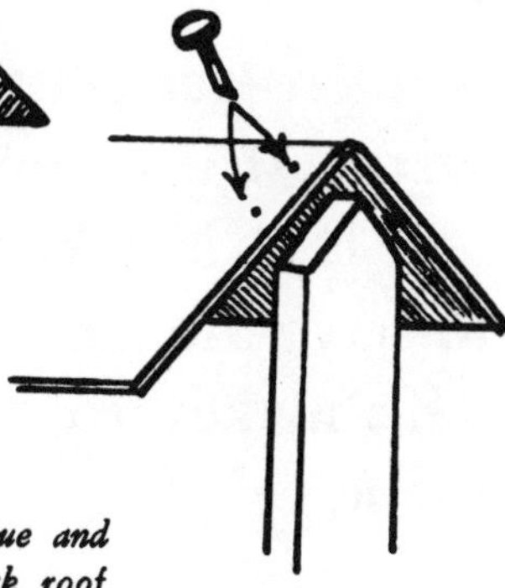

Glue and tack roof to the wood strips.

Special to the Guest of Honor: What To Do When You Are Showered.

When you are led to the surprise corner or room, you should be sincerely grateful to everyone. *Note:* It is your responsibility to show appreciation! Everyone went to all this effort and expense because they like you and want to show their feelings through the shower party. In return, you need to return the feeling of gratitude. Here is the proper way to do it:

1. Open one gift at a time. Read the card containing the name of the donor. Examine the gift.
2. Exclaim happily over the gift, offer a *personal* thank you to the donor, express appreciation of that specific gift, put it aside, with the card intact. (This is important since you will later want to know who gave you the gift.)
3. Don't let your thanks seem "overdone" but try to be genuine in your appreciation.
4. Go on to the next gift and follow the same procedure.
5. Try to make an *individual* comment on each gift so it will not seem too manufactured. *Examples:* If you receive a woolen garment, say that you're happy to have something warm. If it is something to eat, say you'll love to enjoy it with tea. If it is a kitchen appliance, say you're grateful to be able to have the item that will make housework chores much easier. This makes it more personalized and your friends will like you for it.

WRITE A NOTE OF THANKS TO EACH DONOR.

Some folks feel that a verbal "thank you" at the time when the gift is opened at the party is sufficient. But there are many who like to second the "thank you" by a written note. It would be wise for you to do so, sending a little handwritten note as soon as possible, after the shower. A little added token of appreciation is always welcome.

WRITE A THANK YOU NOTE TO THOSE WHO SENT GIFTS.

Any gifts sent by absentee friends who were unable to make a personal appearance because of hardship must be *promptly* acknowledged. Furthermore, as soon as possible, the guest of honor will seek to repay the favor by inviting the guests to her home for a luncheon or dinner (especially if she is a new bride). In your thank you note, be brief. Mention the gift received and express thanks. Use your handwriting for a personal appeal.

THANK THE HOSTESS IN WRITING.

The day after the shower party, write the hostess and express your thanks for having opened her home for the occasion. (Of course, you have voiced your thanks when you attended the party, but a follow-up in writing is considered good taste.)

What to Wear at a Shower.

Your clothes should be in good taste and in keeping with local customs. If the guests favor a certain fashion style, then you should try to dress accordingly. If they frown on certain "fad styles," then it would be wise to refrain from wearing these objectionable clothes. The emphasis here is on the *informal* so your clothes should be casual—but in good taste.

How to Welcome the Extra Guest.

As a hostess, you receive a last-minute telephone call from

a guest who says she is bringing along another guest. You cannot really refuse this extra guest. But since she may not be known to the guest of honor, it would be an imposition to expect her to bring a gift—or for the guest of honor to receive a gift from a stranger. Under these circumstances, the extra guest may be brought along (but *only* when the hostess gives prior permission), and just join in the celebration but without any gifts. *Note:* the extra guest should be one who will fit easily into the group and should not be an outsider or unpleasant type. *Suggestion:* because a shower party is a personal gift-giving affair, guests should refrain from bringing along uninvited and/or unknown friends at the last minute.

How to Welcome an Uninvited Guest.

In the midst of the shower party, the doorbell rings. A familiar caller has arrived. She has *not* been invited to the party but just happened to be in the area and dropped by for a visit. What to do?

Suggestion: Greet the uninvited guest as cordially as though she had been expected. Do not apologize for having omitted her from the party. Just say that there is a shower party in progress and would she care to join in? Make her feel welcome.

If she declines politely, then she should be permitted to leave.

If she accepts the invitation, welcome her inside. *Note:* It is important to tell her about the party since it is inconsiderate to let her come into the festivities without forewarning. After all, she may be too tired or improperly dressed and just wanted to stop by to say a few words. Give her a chance to decline or to accept the invitation. Once she has come into the house, it would be awkward for her to make some excuse to leave. So she should come into the shower party with *willingness,* even if she just happened to come by. Make her feel welcome, let her partake of the festivities and refreshments. She is a guest—gift or not!

What if the Shower Party Must Be Postponed?

A personal and unexpected emergency may make it unavoidably necessary to cancel or postpone a shower party even after the invitations have been mailed and all preparations set up.

The postponement may come because the hostess has a change in plans; or the guest of honor suddenly tells the others she cannot attend the "tea party." In such a case, it is best for the hostess to immediately telephone all guests and tell them there will be a delay.

If gifts have already been delivered, the hostess should hold them and then make an arrangement for another shower party date as soon as possible.

"I've Broken My Engagement!"

If the girl makes this announcement *before* the shower party, then the hostess should immediately notify all the guests who may retrieve their gifts—provided they have not already been given to the engaged girl!

If the girl makes this announcement *after* the shower, the return of the gifts is a matter of personal taste.

Note: The gifts were given and received in good faith. The girl who breaks an engagement should return gifts given to her by her ex-suitor because she wants to terminate his friendship. But she does not want to terminate other friendships. The return of the gifts signifies the end of a friendship. In this situation, the girl will have to "weigh" her friends, perhaps "sound out" a few on the subject and decide accordingly.

Tip: It might be wise for the girl to send notes to all donors saying that she will treasure the gifts that will be kept for the next engagement and shower party.

Personally, if a girl to whom I had given some bath towels as a shower present broke her engagement, I would resent her returning the towels to me! But the girl who feels that her friends *want* their gifts returned will, of course, return them.

Be a Good Hostess-Guest-Honoree

Respect the rights and wishes of others, whether you are the hostess, guest or the guest of honor. Remember that a shower party has been held for the purpose of offering a gift to express friendship. To turn the party into a success, try to be part of each: a hostess, guest and guest of honor. It will help strengthen friendship at a time when it is so important. You may not have a second chance!

4.

Shower Decorations, Refreshments, Games

Decorations

While the emphasis is upon informality, there is no reason why you cannot indulge in well-appreciated elegance in using shower decorations. These decorations need not be elaborate for the informal affair that is the very personality of a shower. But you can help create an immediate air of festivity by using a bouquet of brightly colored flowers, or a pair of lighted candles (for evening showers) on a snowy white tablecloth.

Suggestions: Crepe paper strung in spontaneous manner helps create a "fun decor" mood. Cheerful Chinese lanterns also build a happy mood. Cardboard cut-outs of cartoon characters also help promote a relaxed and informal and tasteful decorative mood.

Note: In deciding on decorations, always keep in mind the *theme* of the shower. (Later chapters offer specific suggestions for individual showers.) For instance, lace and crystal make a lovely background for a silverware shower. Or, bright linen handcloths and towels are suitable for a linen shower. Gaily colored pottery sets the mood for a pottery shower. *Tip:* Con-

MINIATURE UMBRELLA DECORATIONS

The miniature umbrella shown is quite easy and inexpensive to make. When several are placed around on the gift or refreshment table they add much to the mood. The guests will all want one to take home as souvenirs.

Cut the pattern shown above from blue, pink, or yellow construction paper. Draw the detail lines with felt tip pens. Punch the hole in center and then glue area shown.

Now cut a brightly colored pipe cleaner off at a length of 4½ inches. Bend one end around your little finger to form the handle. Apply glue to the inside of the umbrella top, around the punched hole. Now insert the straight end of the pipe cleaner handle. Allow glue to set.

Once the glue has had time to set, take a piece of narrow satin ribbon and tie around the pipe cleaner in a small bow.

← *The finished umbrella.*

sider the guest of honor, too, as you prepare the decorations. A woman business executive might feel out of place when surrounded by dainty pink ribbon bows! An adolescent might feel uncomfortable when surrounded by toys since she wants to consider herself grown up.

You will help create an informal festive mood by using tasteful decorations that fit right in with the *theme.* In succeeding chapters, we offer you specific ideas that should help make your shower a decorative success.

Refreshments

The serving of refreshments is not an all-important part of the shower. But it is considered good taste to provide food that will help make the shower an enjoyable occasion. Refreshments need not put a dent in your budget; a plate of home made cookies with a pitcher of flavorful punch will create a happy atmosphere. Folks may say, "Oh, you shouldn't have gone to all that trouble," when offered a tray of goodies, but you know they've been sniffing eagerly to discover the source of the pleasant kitchen aromas. If you serve satisfying food—whether a cookie or a roast—you will help make your shower a refreshing success!

Tip: Plan your menu carefully, and as far in advance of the shower as practicable. Try to prepare as much food as possible, the night before; or, in the early morning of the day of the shower. *Remember:* hot dishes should be served *hot.* Cold dishes should be served *cold.*

PLAN REFRESHMENTS ACCORDING TO YOUR HOME.

You should adapt your plans to special conditions of your home. Plan a menu that requires a minimum of attention after guests arrive. Pre-arrange all details of service, ready the china, linen, glassware and silverware. Arrange flowers and other accessories such as coasters, ash trays, smoking equipment.

CLEAN YOUR HOUSE.

Your house should look like a shower party! Give it a surface shining. Leave the real big clean-up until after the party. Glass should sparkle, silver should shine. Wash furniture tops; hide precious breakables. Put ash trays and coasters everywhere. This helps ease problems of damage by even the most careful of guests.

YOUR SHOWER PARTY CHECK LIST FOR REFRESHMENTS

After you have planned everything, leave one precious hour for a relaxing hot tub and leisurely dressing. Dress in advance, do some last minute chores. Then you will appear ready if an early guest arrives or you lose track of time. Go down this check list. You may have additional items on your list but be sure to include these:

- ☐ Enough serving dishes; check every food to be served—butter dish, salad bowl, dessert dishes, serving platters, salt and peppers, creamers and sugar bowls.
- ☐ Cups and saucers; one for each guest—large crowds may mean mixed patterns or even rental service.
- ☐ Silverware—enough for each individual service plus serving pieces.
- ☐ Chairs—enough for sit down table service.
- ☐ Tables—depending on type of service—one large or several card tables.
- ☐ Ash trays—you never have too many. Place them everywhere. Saves furniture, rugs, floors.
- ☐ Coasters—you need an abundance.
- ☐ Napkins/placemats/tablecloth—according to menu,

type of service and table. Should be spot- and wrinkle-free.

- ☐ Cigarettes—a favorite brand for your guests' convenience.
- ☐ Centerpiece—order well in advance. Seasonal flowers are more economical.
- ☐ Extra ice cubes—unlimited supply.
- ☐ Pretty hostess apron—need not be practical but must be attractive.
- ☐ Before the party—divide duties between host and hostess if there is a couple in charge.

Four Types of Shower "Meals"

In keeping with the air of informality, there are four types of shower "meals": brunch parties, luncheon parties, buffet supper parties, and dinner parties. Depending upon the size and personality of the shower party, you select the style that is most suited. Of course, a simple buffet at any time of the day is always best for those who wish to treasure the air of informality without becoming too "heavy." After all, a two hour shower party should not be extended to a late-night affair that will wear out the hostess and the guests. Here are four types of shower "meals" and how to help keep your guests refreshed and happy:

BRUNCH PARTIES

This is a wonderful way to entertain because it is so simple and much appreciated. You set the hour much later than breakfast is ordinarily served—but perhaps a bit earlier than lunch. Offer food that will make the proper start for a two-meal day. It may closely resemble a luncheon, although soups and salads seldom are on the menu. Dessert, if any, is usually very light.

Plenty of coffee or tea is a must so keep it hot and handy.

Suggested Brunch Menu. Fresh fruit juice; cheeseburgers *or* scoops of chopped egg or salmon upon rolls; assorted jams and jellies; toast or muffins; coffee and tea.

How To Set The Brunch Table. Deck the table with gay and colorful linen (or cotton, paper, plastic or whatever you like). Your flatware may be the same as you use for every meal. You probably will need just a knife, fork, a couple of teaspoons and a butter knife for each person. Include plain crystal goblets, and a centerpiece of flowers arranged in a small bowl. *Tip:* have a centerpiece with fresh, well-washed fruit. Or, use checked gingham tablecloths with silverware rolled in terrycloth finger-tip towels for napkins that can later be popped into the automatic washer for easy-care. A pewter or brass pitcher filled with garden flowers or even a parsley bouquet with radish roses help make a cheery table.

The Use Of A Lazy Susan. Another help to easy serving in this informal style is the use of a Lazy Susan—either a tray on your buffet table or three-tiered table. On this helpful, revolving object you put sugar, cream, extra butter, the muffin dish, jam, seasonings and all the condiments that ordinarily have to be passed from hand to hand.

LUNCHEON PARTIES

Luncheon shower parties are usually all-female and call for inexpensive entertaining. Light and fancy touches which are so much fun for the hostess are quite appropriate. There are two important points to keep in mind when you give a luncheon shower party: (1) Someone is sure to be late. (2) Someone is sure to be dieting. *What to do to meet these problems:* have a warming tray to keep foods appetizingly hot for late arrivers. Serve salad dressings and meat or dessert sauces *separately* to waistline watchers who can help control calories and eat without fattening sauce.

PAPER BUTTERFLIES

Cut this butterfly from yellow, blue, or pink construction paper. Draw veins and color body with a felt tip pen.

Cut butterfly above from black construction paper. Cut center wing pieces from orange or yellow paper. Glue pieces to wings as shown. Draw vein lines with a felt tip pen.

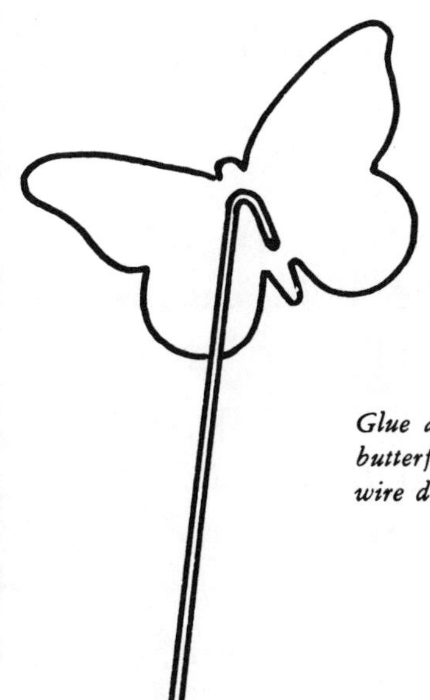

Glue a wire to the back of butterfly as shown. Insert the wire down in flower arrangement.

If desired, bend wire as shown to form a stand.

Suggested Luncheon Menu. Fruit salad; chopped chicken; *or* meat slices; oven-warmed rolls; ice cream or gelatin or pound cake; coffee and tea.

How To Set The Luncheon Table. Use the same linen, glass and china you use at a brunch, but be a little more elegant. Include better china and more elaborate flatware. Table settings may include simple placemats or runners or a lovely tablecloth that will be suitable with your dishes and other accessories as well as the season. Since luncheons are mid-day affairs, candles are *not* used. *Tip:* To put flair on your table, try any of these six centerpiece suggestions: (1) figurines with bowl of delicate greenery and simple flowers as sweet peas, (2) pots of your prize house flowers, (3) low bowl or branches of magnolia or lemon leaves sprayed with silver hair spray, (4) groups of tapered (unlit) candles with flowers or ivy, (5) ivy in a bird cage with colorful paper butterflies, (6) fresh fruit arrangement topped with bunch of frosted grapes.

Include sufficient goblets, cheerful napkins and plenty of ash trays and coasters. No one should have to keep searching and asking for these items.

A Luncheon Party For Men And Women. A luncheon shower party that includes men should be held during the weekend, should provide more substantial fare than one planned for ladies only. *Tip:* If the luncheon party is given in warm weather, guests can carry their full plates to the garden or the terrace, where eating is pleasant and relaxed. *Note:* It is customary to offer *two courses* only at a luncheon shower party. You may have a buffet table with little snacks, though.

BUFFET SUPPER PARTIES

Because the shower party has an emphasis upon informality, a buffet is always most popular. You set up one table upon which everything is placed and guests then partake of the offered fare. *Tip:* arrange the buffet table so that guests can easily take each item in the appropriate order: plates first, followed by entree, vegetable, roll, dessert, beverages. If possible, have a separate table where guests can place their soiled dishes. Always have plenty of silverware and napkins available.

Suggested Buffet Supper Menu. Main dish such as meat, fish, eggs; tossed green salad; bread; pudding or special dessert; coffee, tea, punch.

How To Set A Buffet Supper Party Table. To begin, you make arrangements according to the amount of guests involved.

Example:

1. *For Groups Of 6–8 Guests:* Use a sit-down dinner in your dining area. Or set your table as for a formal dinner but use buffet-style service. You may go fancy and use your best china or keep it casual with simple accessories.
2. *For Groups Of 12–16 Guests:* "Seated" buffet may be the most convenient arrangement. This size group is usually too large to seat at one table. Use small card tables set like a dinner table. Do not crowd guests with a large centerpiece. Instead, a small figurine or demi-tasse cup filled with small flowers is enough. Keep this eating arrangement in mind during the holidays when a large group gathers. Guests serve themselves and select their places. Small groupings help to create an informally intimate and congenial atmosphere.

Additional Suggestions. When the group is too large to serve at "sit-down" formal dinner, the buffet type service is the answer. It can be held in any room in the house or outside on a porch or patio. For outdoor cooking, use a heavy duty extension cord rated for 15 amperes. Do not use ordinary household extension cords. These are too small and will dangerously overheat.

Buffet Benefit. The prime benefit is to have guests serve themselves. Then seat them comfortably and you, the hostess can sit down with the others. All your preparation worries are behind you and all your compliments ahead of you.

Buffet Table Set-ups. Place table with one side against the wall, leaving unlimited space and height for centerpiece arrangements. This layout also eliminates the hazard of anyone tripping on cords from electrical appliances. This set-up makes a U-shape traffic pattern.

Use a dining room table, two small tables together, or an extra folding table. If a larger table is necessary, use two chests of the same height joined by a wide board. Cover the board with cloth reaching to the floor. If your tablecloths are not large enough, use freshly laundered pastel bed sheets. The stripes or floral prints add a refreshing touch to your party setting.

How To Set The Buffet Supper Table. Now, let's decide how to route traffic around the table by setting it so there will be a minimum of confusion. It's important that guests can serve themselves in a logical sequence so that at no time they need to back-track and cause a traffic jam.

Reminder: Rice *before* the curry
Gravy *after* the meat

Arrange food, china and other appointments so they can be picked up in this order.

1. Napkins
2. Dinner Plates (For hot meal, warm plates just as you would for a sit-down dinner.)
3. Cold Dishes (Greens or molded salads.)
4. Hot Foods (Casseroles, meats, etc., on electric warmings, trays, skillets, chafing dishes.)
5. Bread or Rolls
6. Relishes

7. Silver (Placed on the buffet table, unless it is a sit-down buffet.)

Note: Each food should have its own serving silver. Leave enough room near each dish so guests can put down plates to serve themselves easily. Carefully go over every item on the menu, coordinating colors, theme and sequence of table lay-out. To erase all doubts, pick up a plate and make a test run around the table yourself (no nibbling, please) to be sure everything is accessible and in proper order.

HOW TO SERVE DESSERT AT A BUFFET SUPPER TABLE

You may ask a close member of your family to help you clear the buffet table while you reset it for dessert and coffee. You may find it simpler to set up dessert on a side table or bring in a hostess cart. Some hostesses find it easier to serve dessert on trays from the kitchen. *Coffee:* Serve from a coffee table if guests prefer to linger over dessert and coffee in the living room. Finger foods are appropriate to serve at this time.

DINNER PARTIES

Dinner parties are the most elaborate form of shower entertaining. These should also keep an air of informality despite being more elaborate. Gone are the days of ten-course dinners served in great formality with a footman behind every chair. These hardly happen except in the movies and it's a good thing, too. They were always too stifling, self-conscious and never much fun anyway. If the shower guest of honor and occasion calls for a more elaborate affair, then a dinner party is in order—but keep it informal and cheerful.

Suggested Dinner Party Menu. Bowl of hot or cold soup; main meat, fish or egg dish; vegetable platter; bread; cake, pie, meringue or fancy dessert; coffee or exotic beverage.

How To Set The Dinner Party Table. Silver is to be placed

in the order it is used. Spoons and knives are placed on the right of dinner plate; sharp knife edges face plate. Dinner and salad or dessert fork is placed to left of the plate. The dessert and coffee silver may be placed with the initial setting to save time. Left of the dinner plate, above the forks, place the bread and butter plate with butter spreader square on the dish. Water glass is placed to the right of plate above the knife. If coffee is to be served with the main course, place cups with handles out from plates. Have place mats, a sturdy tablecloth, napkins, candles, various salt and pepper accessories. Individual sets go between every two places. Ash trays are placed above dinner plate or to the right of the spoons. *Tip:* Candles for a dinner party are white or cream if it is a formal occasion for a very special shower guest. If it is an informal occasion, any color may be used. Candles should *not* be on the table unless they are to be lighted—and not lighted unless the room is dark. Keep flame above eye level.

Suggestions. Set the table well before the arrival of the guests. A serving cart with two tiers is almost indispensable to the hostess. This helps ease endless trips to and from the kitchen which may be disturbing to the party and to your feet, too!

Dinner Is Served. You should have the first course on the table when the guests come into the dining room. If it's cold food, there's nothing to worry about. If it's hot soup, it should be served either in covered dishes or from a tureen so that it will still be hot when guests start to eat. *Note:* Put as many of the dishes for the main course on your serving cart as possible. A casserole, for instance, wrapped in a large napkin and well covered should keep hot for half an hour.

How To Have Guests Help Without Really Trying. Here is one system that I saw used at an elegant dinner shower party that called for the help of the guests and they loved it!

The main course, in its serving dishes, is put on the sideboard or buffet or hot trays accompanied by hot plates. After the first course has been removed, guests rise and serve themselves, bringing their plates back to the table. Guests not only enjoy doing this, but they get their hot food quickly. They help out without really trying and the air of informality is improved!

HOW TO PLAN A SUCCESSFUL SHOWER MENU

Whether simple or elaborate, proper menu planning means much toward a successful shower. Use only foods that you can easily serve and your kitchen equipment can accommodate. Don't "experiment" when you entertain. And, it's a good idea to "rehearse" once or twice at a family meal. If you have a special recipe for which you are famous, feel free to use it; your guests may be looking forward to it. Here are 8 tips to help speed success in planning a shower menu:

1. Avoid repetition. If tomato juice is the appetizer, don't use tomato sauce in the main dish.
2. Try to maintain a balance between solid and soft foods.
3. Flavors should harmonize or contrast but should not compete.
4. Don't serve too many starches (potatoes, bread, rice) at one meal.
5. Foods should have a variety of colors, textures and sizes to give eye appeal to the overall arrangement.
6. Plan the menu with some regard for food likes, dislikes, allergies of guests, if you know them. If in doubt, keep it simple.
7. Start menu planning around one important dish that can be partially or completely prepared ahead of time and served in its cooking utensil.
8. For buffet service, select food that can be eaten with a

fork and a minimum amount of cutting. Avoid gooey sauces and gravies. Plan desserts so that guests can help themselves; try finger food that can easily be handled.

Games

Some people like games at shower parties. Other prefer to sit around and chat and just share good friendship. It is best to keep in mind the personal preferences of the guests and also the *theme.* If the group prefers to look over the gifts, pass them around for admiration, then keep games down to a minimum. If the *theme* of the shower calls for games, it would be good to have a few available, for those who want to play games.

Note: There are times when the party mood fails and conversation falters. A good hostess is alert for a lull and then brings out a few games and *gently* suggests participation. No one should be forced into a game.

Packaged games for adults are available in almost all party goods shops, department stores, various other outlets. Select a few of them and just spread them out and let those who voluntarily seek participation, enjoy games among themselves.

Caution: Keep the informal air even with games. To say suddenly, "Quiet, everyone! We're going to play a game!" is much like blowing a referee's whistle. Your guests will respond to the informal shower atmosphere if you *suggest* a game, rather than command one.

In the following chapters, we suggest various games that will fit in with the *theme* of the shower.

Odds and Ends.

It is regarded as good shower etiquette for the hostess to

welcome her guests at the door. She may designate someone else to do so while she circulates among those already arrived, making them comfortable. Each guest should be led immediately to a room where she may remove her wraps. Then she is brought to join the others and drawn into whatever activity they have begun. The "Surprise, Surprise" should not be heard until (naturally) the guest of honor has arrived and the other guests are all assembled and their gifts placed in the "hiding spot." If there are a few latecomers and time is running out, then do not overstrain the guests. Have the "Surprise, Surprise" cry and the offering of the "hidden" gifts to the guest of honor. Latecomers can make amends when they arrive.

Important: The hostess should know that *the party begins with the first arrival.* Give your earliest guest or guests something to do right away, even if it is just looking around, noting the arrangements, etc. *Never* leave your first guest sitting stiffly in a chair, wishing she had not been so punctual.

In summation, have a wonderful time!

5.

The Bride-To-Be Shower

The most popular shower is that for the bride-to-be. To honor a young woman who is getting married is a longtime tradition and it's also a very practical way to help her get ready to set up housekeeping. To help made a bride-to-be shower a happy success, here are some important tips:

1. *When to give a bridal shower.* Showers are usually given about a month before the wedding. Consult with others so that the girl has one or two different showers at the very most. It is best for donors to join together for *one* shower; one group shower given about one month before the event is best and more economical.

2. *Who gives a bridal shower.* Any close friend gives the bridal shower. Usually, it is a member of the bridal party, if there is to be one. Often, the shower is given by the maid or matron of honor if she is *not* a sister or other close relative, and if she lives in the community and has the facilities for entertaining as a hostess. *Note:* bridal showers are not to be given by members of the families of bride or groom.

3. *Try to keep it a surprise.* Showers are a "surprise" to the bride who supposedly has no idea that when she is invited to a tea or luncheon, that she will be gift-showered. It is wise to quietly consult her as to her needs and also her size, if personal wearing apparel is to be given.

4. *A bridal shower can be inexpensive.* Shower gifts can be inexpensive and economical because her closest friends will probably give her more costly gifts at the actual wedding.

5. *Always bring a gift.* Guests at the bridal shower always bring a gift. Because only the closest friends are invited to the bridal shower, it is a slight if someone does not show up but mails the gift, or shows up without a gift.

6. *The groom is absent.* The groom should be absent from the bridal shower. But he need not be neglected. He can be given separate gifts at a "groom shower" or else, invited guests may bring separate gifts addressed to him to be opened himself at a later date. (*Note:* At a bridal shower, it could be embarrassing if the girl opens up a box of intimate lingerie while the groom is standing about, hence the suggestion that the groom be absent at such affairs.)

Invitations:

Notepaper shaped like wedding bell, sketches of bride and groom, bridal veil, horseshoe for good luck, hope chest and other wedding-related themes.

Decorations:

Use wedding bells, cupids with bows, hearts and flowers (especially orange blossoms), paper slippers filled with rice, watering pots with silver ribbons streaming from the spouts, little cheerful-colored parasols from which hang flowers or ribbons or bright confetti. Also, carry out the specific shower theme.

Gift Ideas

If there is no specific theme (these will follow in this chapter,) then you might have a general theme of just about anything the bride-to-be can use. Suggested gifts include: hosiery, lingerie, fittings for the dressing table, towels, bath mats, shower curtains, linens, little pieces of pottery and even jars of jams and jellies, hatstands, shoe racks, patio and garden fixtures and garden tools, games, playing cards, phonograph records, outdoor items such as thermos bottles, sandwich cases, baskets and travel equipment. Handy gadgets for the kitchen and bath are always welcome.

Entertainment

Try word games, scrabble, famous dates, mah jongg sets, wedding quiz games and packaged games. Keep these to a minimum since the bride-to-be has so much to do that she will be too worn out with games.

Food Suggestions

If this is an afternoon and informal affair, have cookies, perhaps one big cake that is sliced up and enjoyed by all, small candies and goodies. Include lots of hot coffee, tea and punch. If this is a more involved shower, then have more ample food such as a buffet.

The Linen Shower

Send invitations on paper towels. Decorate with small paper towel place cards beside paper plates. Use cloth napkins. *Gift suggestions for the linen shower:* no-iron percales, tea towels, guest towels, bath towels, bedsheets, pillowcases, bedspread, doilies, dishcloths, tablecloth, place mats, napkins, washcloths, bathroom set, toaster cover, curtains (if you know correct size).

The Chinaware Shower

Send invitations in the shape of a teacup; you might cut various colored construction paper in this shape, writing your invitation in front. To decorate, cover the gift table with white paper that has pasted pictures of dishes and glassware cut out from newspapers or magazines. A hodge-podge of such pictures creates an interesting effect.
Gift suggestions for the chinaware shower: cup and saucer set, dinner plate, tureen, vegetable dish, salad dish, gravy boat, soup bowls, dessert dishes, salt and pepper shakers, large fruit or punch bowl, sugar-and-cream set, parfait glasses, goblets, candy dish, snack tray, relish dish, condiment set, candleholders, bud vase, punch ladle, crystal cooler, ice bucket.

The Kitchen Shower

Write invitations on a slender sheet of white paper (about three inches wide and ten inches long); wrap around and fasten with a colored toothpick. You will need to deliver these personally; or else, flatten and insert in envelope for mailing. To decorate, try to have your shower in the kitchen which is an appropriate atmosphere! *Tip:* Use a very large kettle put on the kitchen table and all gifts inserted within or around, if there is an overabundance. Fasten gaily colored ribbons to the handles to give a cheerful atmosphere.
Gift suggestions for the kitchen shower: soup tureen, cheeseboard, revolving relish server, casserole, fondue forks, oriental dinner gong, saucepans, fry pan, broiler and rotisserie, vertical broiler, corn popper, baker-broiler, toaster-broiler, combination grill and waffle iron, waffle baker, blender, ice making machine, stainless steel mixing bowl set, electric or manual can opener, hand mixer, whistling tea kettle, electric coffee

maker, electric appliance timer, pressure cooker, cookie sheets, muffin tins, kitchen clock, spatula-and-spoon set, hamburger press, spice shelf, potato masher, knife holder, spoons, forks, knives, canister set.

The Trousseau Shower

Write invitations on a diary page and insert guest of honor's name on top. Scallop edges of pink paper to give a feminine effect. Sprinkle with sachet and handwrite the data. To decorate, obtain several books of cut out paper dolls from a five-and-ten store; or make your own from magazine figures. Dress in delicate and feminine attire and scatter around the room and on the gift and refreshment tables.

Gift suggestions for the trousseau shower: gown, peignoir, half slip, negligee, vanity bench items, hosiery, costume jewelry, sachet, bride's book, diary, perfume, cosmetics, bed jacket, handkerchiefs, bedroom slippers, panty set, gloves, sandals, house slippers, culottes, hostess robe, duster, quilted duster or wrapper, nylon tricot granny gown, pantyhose.

The "Anything Goes" Shower

Use ordinary white paper; paste on pictures from magazines of typical shower gifts. Anything goes! This can be a shower with the theme for the kitchen, living room, bedroom, travel or whatever. On the front of invitation, put down "Anything Goes" so invited guests know they have complete freedom of choice. To decorate, use crepe-paper streamers attached to an open umbrella, or use an ordinary corrugated packing carton with affixed ribbons to give a "helter-skelter" appearance. In this carton, the gifts are placed.

Gift suggestions for the "Anything Goes" shower: steak knives, candle snuffer, clock, lamp, bathroom scales, picture frame, ice tongs, barbecue set, cosmetic set, small vases, hamper, Bible, rolling pin, canisters, food and vegetable cutter, electric slicer, pepper mill, paper holder, turntables, still-life wall plaques, key case, lingerie, a pair of tickets to a forthcoming play, a gift certificate at a local department store, a set of books, inexpensive transistor radio, record album or an individual and economical single record.

The Home Furnishing Shower

Write invitations on paper that is made in the shape of a house; or, obtain sketches of door knobs or door knockers from leading house magazines and paste upon the paper. To decorate, put a large dollhouse in the center of the gift table. If you cannot borrow one from a little girl, then make one out of cardboard and use a little red brick (match box) for a chimney. Artistry is not important since this is a "fun" shower and the "wilder" your drawing, the more entertaining it will be.

Gift suggestions for a home furnishing shower: clock radio, brass mailbox, bedspread, tables and small furniture items, picture, blanket, door chimes, lamp, magazine rack, starter set of dishes or cookware, stainless steel set of tableware or cutlery, phonograph, record cabinet, portable stereo, folding chairs and card table, ashtray set, cigarette table, room dividers, stack stools, floor cushion, wall plaques, two-tier knick knack shelf, andirons, umbrella stand, fireplace bellows, end table, small hassock, spinning wheel planter.

His and Hers Bridal Showers

If you want to honor both the bride and groom, then you may hold a special "his and hers" bridal shower. It would be

HOME FURNISHING INVITATION

Cut the pattern from heavy white paper.

Fold the invitation as shown below.

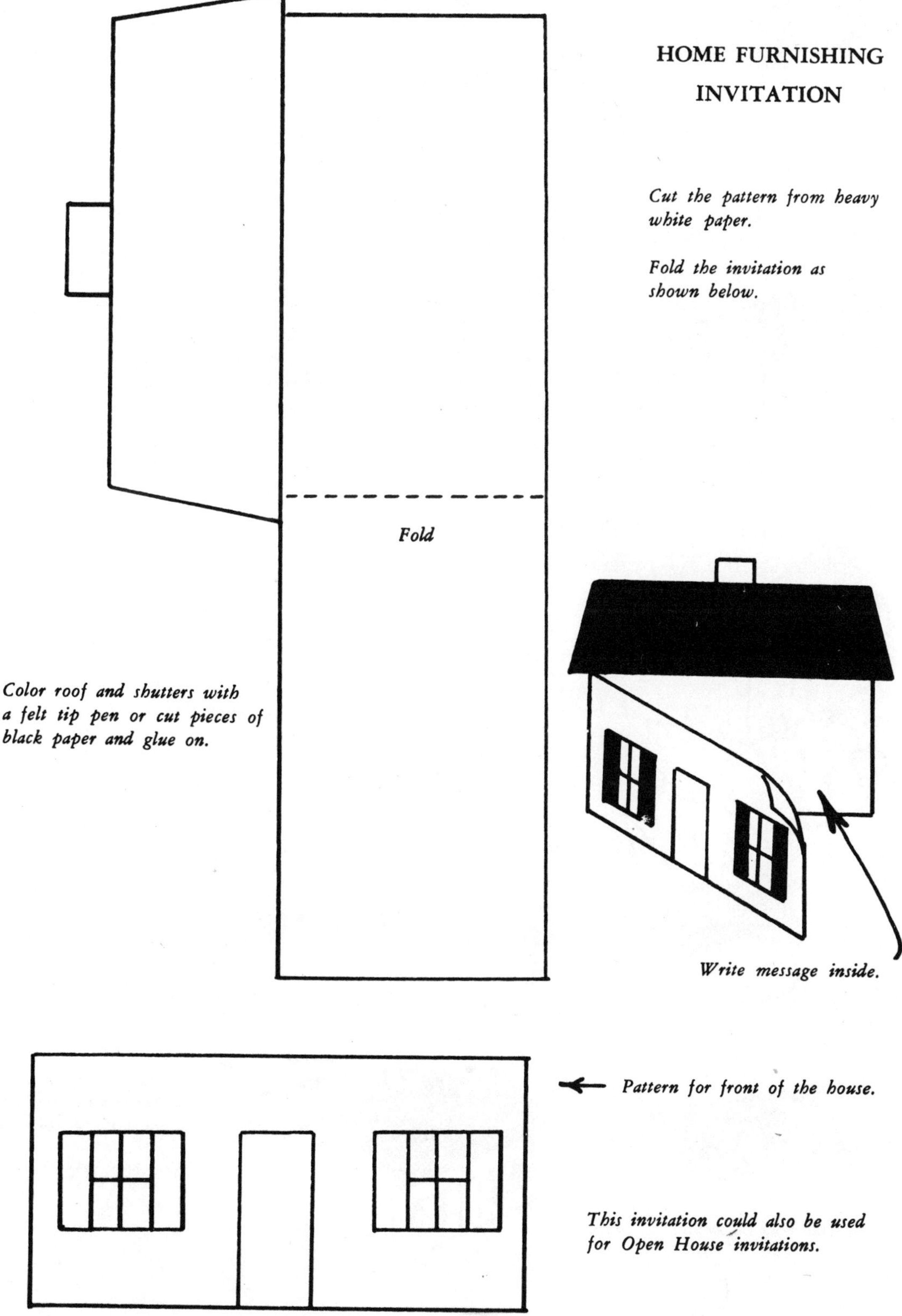

Color roof and shutters with a felt tip pen or cut pieces of black paper and glue on.

Write message inside.

Pattern for front of the house.

This invitation could also be used for Open House invitations.

DOLLHOUSE DECORATION

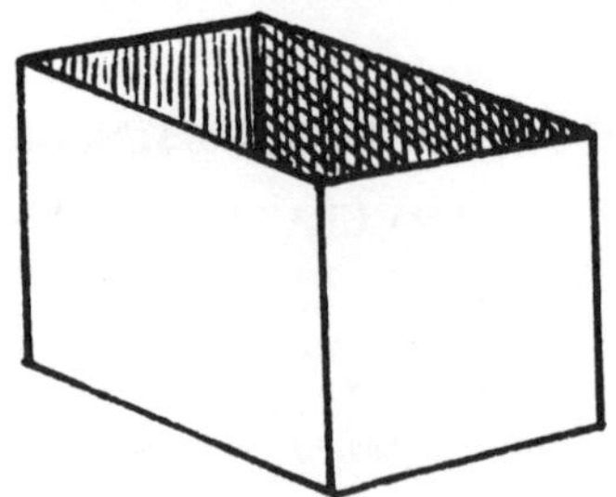

If no little girl's dollhouse is available, make your own.

First you will need a rectangular shaped cardboard box. The size will depend upon how large a house you desire.

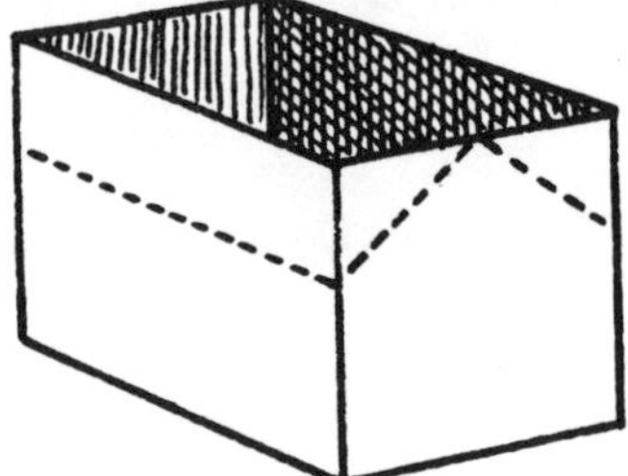

Mark the gable ends, front and back as shown. Use these lines as a guide and cut with scissors or a sharp knife. If a knife is used, be careful.

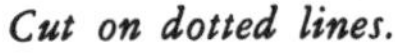

Cut on dotted lines.

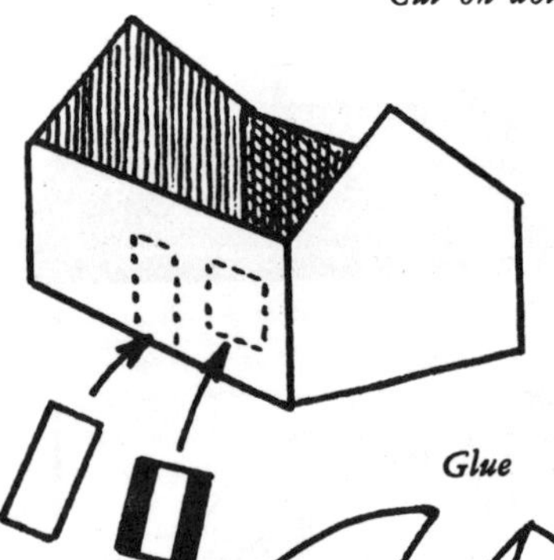

The box should now be shaped as the one pictured. The next step is to paint the box with a latex type house paint or cover it with colored paper. Once this has been done, cut a door and windows from construction paper and glue on house.

Glue

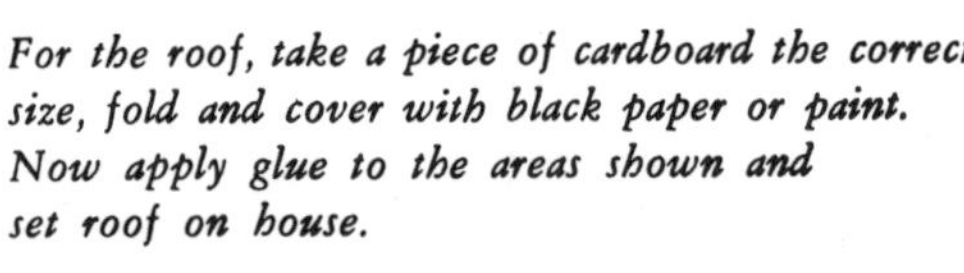

For the roof, take a piece of cardboard the correct size, fold and cover with black paper or paint. Now apply glue to the areas shown and set roof on house.

Use a match box or folded cardboard for the chimney.

Glue roof on house.

wise for all invited guests to get together and plan, in advance, the types of gifts offered so there will be no embarrassment over opening up a gift containing intimate apparel. Write invitations on plain white 4 x 6 inch cards, folded in half. You might use pasted drawings of "his and hers" towels to explain that both will attend the surprise shower. *Tip:* You might add something like this at the bottom of the invitation:

Are you a "He"? Bring a gift for "him."

Are you a "She"? Bring a gift for "her."

To decorate, use double items—example, an apron with a pair of overalls, a golf club with a rolling pin, a feminine glove with a masculine glove, feminine bedroom slipper with a man's work shoe, a frilly handkerchief with a bow tie. Have one large gift table, divided in half; one side should be covered with pink paper, the other side with blue paper and this is self-explanatory as to where gifts should be placed. The bride-to-be opens her gifts on the pink side of the table, thanks the donor and shares admiration with the groom-to-be. He opens his gifts on the blue side of the table, thanks the donor and shares admiration with the bride-to-be. *Note:* we emphasize the need for pre-selection so as not to have either bride-to-be or groom open up an embarrassingly intimate gift.

Gift suggestions for a His and Hers bridal shower:

HIS:
hammer, chef's hat and apron, tiepin, travel alarm clock, auto tools, wrench, robe, shaving equipment, pen-and-pencil set, record albums, wallet, camera, money clip, comb-and-brush set, trouser hangers, pipe, framed auto or hunting prints, cufflinks.

HERS:
clothing storage bag, fluffy slippers, cookbook, cosmetic kit, hairdryer, perfume, soap, apron, owl bank, kerchief, egg timer, pot holders, gloves, tickets to a good play, small clutch bag, change holder, nailpolish.

The Money Shower

For the girl who has everything, there is always the need for more money. Money is a delicate subject; a shower of the "green stuff" is certainly welcome since you can never go wrong by giving money—it's the one gift no one ever returns!! But it may be offensive if the guest of honor has the attitude this is a monetary obligation. It is best to gather the guests together and decide if it is appropriate to offer money. It is especially suitable if the bride-to-be is on the move, has to travel with her husband, does not have a home to be furnished, or just needs money! Telephone invitations would be best. This helps eliminate misunderstandings. Explain that you are holding a "money shower" for so-and-so, give the time and place, and suggest that because of her personal circumstances, a little gift of money would be most appreciated so that the bride-to-be may later select her own purchase when she is settled. All invited guests put money in a gift envelope bearing their names and give to the hostess who holds it until the shower. To decorate, use a simple table. You might want to take an ordinary egg carton, and fold each envelope within each little pocket. To add an effect, decorate the carton with scraps of satin, tulle and lace. Place a shirt cardboard painted with a stained-glass motif or a wedding picture cut out from a magazine, right behind the box. This creates a romantic and colorful effect for offering money.

Gift suggestions for a money shower: money is money and "green stuff" cannot be decorated, but it can be wrapped in gaily colored tissue gift wrap and inserted in cheerful looking envelopes. *Note:* to take the "edge" off the somewhat "cold" gift of money, here's a suggestion—each guest writes a little charming 4-line verse on a slip of colored paper and inserts with the money. When the bride-to-be opens each envelope, she reads the verse and thanks the donor for the charming inspirational message and the money. This enables her to make a *personal* thank you for the money by referring to the verse.

The Silver Shower

For invitations, use silver-edged note paper; or, paste cutouts on any silverware on a large sheet of paper, fold over and handwrite the details. To decorate, emphasize the silver theme. Cover a table with aluminum foil to give a silver effect; or, wrap cups in foil and fill with refreshments after all have arrived. All gifts, wrapped in silver foil are placed upon the foil-covered table.

Gift suggestions for a silver shower: gravy boat, tureen, salt and pepper shakers, coffee or tea service, candy dish, relish dish, gourmet set, bread tray, spoons, forks, cutlery, gravy ladle, meat fork, butter dish, shrimp forks, demitasse spoons, silver-plated soap dish and tumbler for the bathroom, candlesticks, platter, bud vase, goblet, cake plate, pitcher. *Note:* Because this calls for more costly gifts, it is best to include only those guests who are very close to the bride.

The Bathroom Shower

The theme here is to bring bathroom gifts. Your invitation could be an elaborate handwritten message in bright green crayon on a white correspondence card which is draped in green cellophane to give the effect of a real shower and curtain. Draw or paste a picture of a bath towel on a rack across the top. To decorate, use the same color theme by putting a huge clothes hamper in the center of the room, then put crepe paper and ribbons onto the lid.

Gift suggestions for a bathroom shower: vanity stool with

fluffy seat cover, shower curtain, metal cabinet with mirrored sliding door, wall shelf, bath scale, scatter rug, wicker hampers, wall magazine rack, cordless automatic toothbrush, bathtub grab bar, water spray toothbrush, mix-and-match towel set, plastic curtains, lotion bottles, tissue containers, luxury soaps, bath oils, bath mitts, automatic soap dispenser, hair brush, clothes brush, facial mist, hair dryer, lighted cosmetic case.

The Book Shower

Send invitations in the shape of a book; make your own by folding a piece of paper into a tiny book size object. Write out the invitation and set the theme by suggesting that anything that is a "book" is acceptable. To decorate, set aside a table that is decorated with cut outs from the Sunday book section of your newspaper.

Gift suggestions for a book shower: In keeping with the theme, you should consider book-shaped compacts, toiletries in book containers, and book-like cigarette boxes. Book matches with embossed names, address books, stationery in handy book form. Any popular or rather less-than-popular book is advisable; cookbooks, magazine subscriptions and even a pre-paid subscription for a one year membership in a book club.

The Breakfast Shower

This is convenient and very informal and may be held any available morning. Invitations can contain tiny clock faces with the exact hour marked in red. Decorations should be a table covered with various items used as breakfast equipment. Serve breakfast to your guests and the guest of honor and have lots of gabby fun together.

Gift suggestions for a breakfast shower: inexpensive orange juicers, grapefruit knives, egg timers, spatulas, griddle and waffle irons, muffin tins or several boxes of attractively designed novelty paper napkins. For more expensive tastes, there would be glass coffee makers, double boilers for cooking hot cereals on chilly mornings, custard cups, breakfast cloths, place mats, cheerfully colored napkins, also a breakfast cookbook, a handy complete breakfast service for two and a small collection of assorted jams and jellies.

The Paper Gifts Shower

To emphasize the paper theme, use newsprint upon which you paste the invitations. This is usually suitable for luncheon. Decorations could include brightly colored paper streamers, paper doilies, paper parasols. As a receptacle in which to place paper gifts—have a huge shopping bag that has been decorated with ribbons and bows.

Gift suggestions for a paper shower: lace paper doilies, extra large paper napkins, paper hat box, paper lunch cloths, paper fingertip towels, bizarre stationery, correspondence cards, menu pads, long paper fireplace matches, playing cards, personally printed colorful stationery, the new paper garments (be sure to know the size in advance), various paper disposable items.

The Can Shower

To make appropriate thematic invitations, cut sizable colored pictures of canned foods from advertisements and paste upon correspondence cards or larger pieces of white cardboard. To decorate, have all food served as canned; tea and coffee come in cans, too. As a centerpiece in which canned gifts are to be placed, try a large oversized basket. The basket, as well as the canned foods, should be given to the bride-to-be.

Gift suggestions for a can shower: anything that comes in a can, including food, clothing, pencils, washing fluids, soaps, paints, candy, cake, meats, fish, preserved foods. Try to have a variety.

The Clean Sweep Shower

From a mop or broom, take some strings and straws, paste to a large card and announce a "clean sweep" shower. Gifts call for everything that is used for cleaning. To decorate, have a huge wash basin or miniature tub that is colorfully arranged with ribbons and bows, standing atop a washboard on a table. In this basin, all cleaning gifts are placed.

Gift ideas for a clean sweep shower: a carpet sweeper, window brush, broom, mop, electric cleaner, jars of cleaning fluid, silver polish, floor wax, tea towels, wash cloths, cotton and rubber cleaning gloves, a jar of cleansing cream, various soaps and powders, clothespins.

The Hot Bread Shower

Paste assorted bread recipes and photos of bread and baking items onto a piece of white paper that is cut into the shape of a slice of bread. To decorate, have different types of baked goods that are served to guests—here is one decoration that they can eat, too!

Gift suggestions for a hot bread shower: electric griddle, waffle iron, toaster, sandwich grill, bread cookbook, bread recipe file, muffin tins, cornbread tins, popover pans, custard cups, pastry brush, biscuit cutters, pan holders.

The Knotty Shower

The unique idea here is that all gifts are knotted up. Your

invitation could be a simple note paper that is tied up with a knotty string that has to be opened in order for the invitation to be read. Decorations could include all sorts of knotty things around the table.

Gift ideas for a knotty shower: knotty bath towels and washcloths, knotty guest and fingertip towels, small bathroom string rugs, bowknot-patterned linens, slippers with strings knotted together, robes with sash knotted around. *Note:* much of the fun here is that all the knots *must* be untied—not cut or broken!

The Spicy Shower

The theme here is to give gifts containing spices and herbs. Reflect the theme in the invitation by using Xerox-copied old woodcuts (check your library for reference works) upon which you write the details. Decorations could be enlarged Xerox-copied woodcuts, old sailing ships, scenic views of islands to suggest locale of growing spices and herbs.

Gift ideas for a spicy shower: anything from a spicily scented lingerie outfit to tiny containers of rare spices, spiced cookies, perfumes, bath powders, colognes, spicy sachet sets, spice cook book, spicy candies and confections, kitchen canisters containing little bottles of cooking spices, wearing apparel with spice colors.

The Personal Shower

This shower should include only the bride-to-be and her very personal friends because it calls for giving intimate and personal gifts. The invitation could be in a blushing pink, perhaps a sketch of an embarrassed little girl, or lipstick imprints, or a winking eye. Decorations should reflect the dainty and intimate such as a lacy tablecloth in a very pink color.

SHOWER INVITATION DESIGNS

Silver Shower

Spicy Shower

Breakfast Shower

Clean Sweep Shower

Gift ideas for a personal shower: lingerie, undergarments, hosiery, toiletries, creams and lotions, frilly bed robe, brassiere, nylon tricot slip, half or full slip, briefs, panty hose, blouse, peignoir set, delicate blouse, knee-high ribbed stockings, frilly hostess robe, toga, pleated gown, jump suit, pajama set, female products.

The Tea Shower

Benefit here is that this calls for an informal arrangement and need not involve much effort. Invitations could be tea-colored. In each envelope, slip a small tea bag that the invited guest can use. Decorate the house with photos of tea plants, old time tea ships, tea kettles.

Gift ideas for a tea shower: everything that goes with the serving of tea. This could include tea kettle, pourer, tea cups, chinaware, a tea table, small boxes of tea balls or packages of tea, a silver tea ball, dainty tea napkins, conventional linen tea napkins, a lemon fork, sugar-creamer set, a tea cookbook, pitcher for iced tea, sets of tumblers and matching jugs.

The Basic Rules for a Fool-Proof Bride-To-Be Shower

To prepare a fool-proof bride-to-be shower, here is a set of rules to follow. No mistakes, if you follow these steps in programmed sequence:

1. First, check the date with the guest of honor or someone close to her. Brides have hectic schedules and must plan their time carefully.

2. Plan to give the shower from two to four weeks before the wedding. *Remember:* only friends give showers; relatives may have parties for the prospective bride, but gifts are not given.

3. Try to have a surprise shower; if not, go over your guest list with the betrothed. All close friends should be included.

4. Send out invitations at least two weeks before the shower party date.

5. Plan a swift-paced shower of about two hours—that way, no one feels obligated to stay longer. Naturally, if everyone is having fun, don't cut the party short. If you're planning on playing games at the shower, limit them to one or two brief ones. If there are lots of gifts, have her open them while the guests are enjoying their refreshments.

6. If you can't decide on a theme, then one that emphasizes housewares is always welcome. You can include a set of measuring cups, a set of food keepers, a meat thermometer, a dish drainer, an onion chopper. New cooks always can use spatulas, turners and ladles. Gifts that make more storage space in cabinets, like revolving turntables, storage bins and slide-out drawers are sure to please any bride-to-be.

7. A simple decorative idea is to use colored crepe paper, lots of ribbons, little objects and novelties. Take a large wicker basket, decorate it with ribbons and use it for holding the wrapped gifts. The guest of honor gets to keep the basket, too.

Note: Often, friends are economically pinched and are unable to pay for the arrangements. While these do not cost much, they may be a hardship upon the hostess and her friends. Under these circumstances, the engaged girl's sister or mother may contribute something to pay for the expenses—but all invitations should be sent out in the friend's name and the shower held at the friend's home.

6.
The Wedding Shower

There is one particular rule to this shower—it must be held *after* the wedding. It is a postnuptial shower which friends want to hold to show their affection for the young couple. It may be held whether or not there was a bride-to-be shower. It need not be held at all, and it depends upon the individual circumstances. The wedding shower may be held in the evening or on weekends since it calls for a husband guest-of-honor and a wife guest-of-honor and both should be present. Again, good taste is essential so that delicate gifts do not offend either husband or wife since both will open gifts in full view of everyone.

You may hold the shower at the home of the married couple, but arrange the date in advance. You would not want to catch them unawares. If you wish to keep it as a "surprise," then tell them that you and several others would like to stop by on (specify date and time) and chat with them about newly married life. Or, just send them an invitation to come to the house of the hostess and specify it is to be a tea or luncheon and they will have a reserved place. This impresses them with the importance of the date and they will be sure to keep it.

Invitations: Clip pictures of wedding rings, tied knots, rice, shoes and other marital decorations, to small cards and write down the time and place and whether or not it is to be a surprise.

Decorations: A simple bulletin board is cheerful when decorated with little cartoons of husband-wife experiences or problems. Try a rolling pin decorated with a large bow. Or take brown paper bags and paste wedding pictures on the outside and fill these with the gifts.

Gift ideas: Emphasize the practical here. Include food such as cans of coffee or tea, shortening, packaged cake mix, canned fruits and vegetables, spice containers, bouillon cubes, any packaged foods, recipes, cookbooks, exotic imported foods.

Entertainment: Try any packaged games, or guessing games. Here's a thought: write down on slips of paper the names of famous couples—the name of the wife on one piece, and the name of the husband on the other. Each wife picks out one slip of paper from a special bowl and tries to guess who the famous husband should be. Each husband picks out his slip of paper and tries to match up the wife. Then, when all have their slips of paper, it's fun to see who "married" who.

For refreshments, try various types of homemade cakes, cookies and yummy confections. Lots of coffee, tea and punch, too. A fool-proof combination is sweet apple cider with a basketful of doughnuts.

7.

The Baby Shower

It is always a joyous occasion to participate in a stork shower. Everyone loves to prepare gifts for the soon-to-arrive. This type of shower calls for gifts that are meant to be worn and used by the baby. Its very theme limits you *only* to gifts that are to be used by the baby in one form or another.

Note: A baby shower is usually for the *first* baby born to the couple and not a strict rule for all other following blessed events. But if you feel inclined to greet succeeding new arrivals then you should certainly do so.

A baby shower is given *after* the birth of the baby, not before. Only intimate women friends of the new mother participate in the shower. It should be given during the day, possibly at a lunch or a tea party. The guests all bring gifts for the baby. In some communities, such showers are disapproved of, so be sure that the mother for whom you plan it will not be offended.

Gifts include clothes and other baby items and also money. Gifts of money for the baby's account are presented to the mother in cash, check or bond, enclosed in gift cards. A baby's bond is made out to the child and his mother.

Invitations to baby showers may be made by telephone or printed message, about one month before the arrival of the

BABY SHOWER MOTIFS

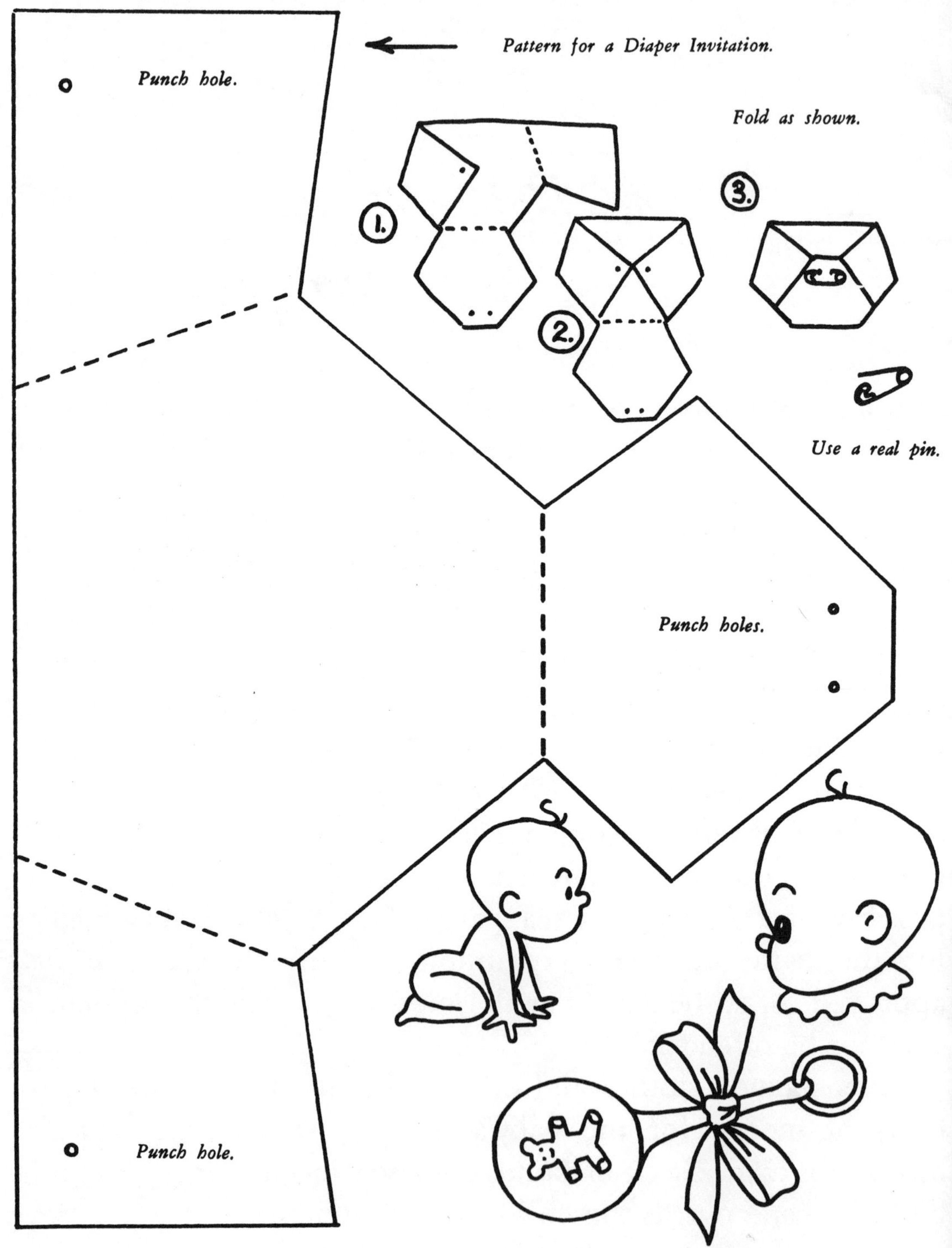

child. If, for some reason, the stork delays, then you postpone the shower until the arrival. And, the mother sends thank you notes to all donors.

Here are variations of the baby shower.

Baby Book Motif

The invitations should resemble a baby record book; just a few sketches of a baby face, or some bowknots with the words, "baby record book" on the front, will give the idea. Wrap all gifts in either light blue or pink (depending upon boy or girl), with lovely cutout flowers or garlands pasted on top.

Gift ideas for a baby book motif: an attractive picture frame, a small instamatic camera, any article of clothing, a tiny soft toothbrush, a toy, an infant weight and height chart, a bath thermometer, soft baby washcloths, infant soap and even bath toys, or a bankbook with a small sum as a "first birthday" starter.

Baby Wardrobe Shower

Cut letter paper into the shape of diapers, write your messages in the center, fold in triangular manner, fasten with safety pins. This informs the guests it is to be a wardrobe shower. Decorations consist of little baby clothes on an indoor clothesline; take a white laundry hamper and decorate with either blue or pink ribbons and streamers. Place all gifts inside the hamper which is opened by the guest at the moment of "surprise, surprise!" The hamper, too, is a gift that she takes with her.

Gift ideas for a baby wardrobe shower: crib sheets, diapers, diaper pins, rattle, bonnet, kimono, shirts (long and short sleeves), washcloths, bunting, quilt, disposable diapers, plastic diaper covers, gown, receiving blanket, mittens, crawler, terry cloth bathrobe.

Mother Goose Shower

This offers a bright novelty shower in which everything is planned around the nursery rhyme motif. Invitations should have Mother Goose decorations. Decorations should include dolls and toys and games that use the Mother Goose theme. These decorations may also serve as gifts to be taken by the mother.

Gift ideas for a Mother Goose shower: tiny nursery lamps with Little Boy Blue or Bo-Peep bases, Mother Goose and nursery rhyme books, Mother Goose pictures, bibs decorated with nursery rhyme designs, small kimonos with similar design, tiny cushions on which Jack jumps over the candlestick and small rugs and infant bath notions with appropriate decorations.

Suggestion: for refreshments, serve animal crackers, home made cookies cut in the shape of fairy tale characters, ducks, gingerbread men.

Baby Treasure Chest Shower

Small treasure chests can be used for holding the gifts. The chests, too, are given to the mother who can use them for storing objects. Invitations could be shaped like treasure chests, decorated with bits of colored tape in jewel shapes. The invitation emphasizes that this shower is to "fill a baby treasure chest" and followed with specific time and place.

Decorations could consist of a large wooden orange crate or large box which is filled with all the treasure chests and gifts. Pink or blue streamers and colored ribbons and, perhaps, a few balloons, decorate the box.

Gift ideas for a baby treasure chest shower: silver rattle, baby powder, baby lotion, booties, silver cup, cotton swabs, baby soap and shampoo, towels, formula pitcher, nipples, spoon, frame for baby's hospital bracelet, gift certificates, washcloths, rubber pads, quilt.

Pink or Blue Baby Shower

The theme depends upon whether the stork brought a girl or boy. Everything, from invitations to gifts, should reflect the color. Your invitation should be of pink or blue construction paper cut in the shape of a cradle, or a rattle. Decorations consist of a real infant's cradle or bassinet (which is given to the mother) with the appropriate color. You might add an appropriate doll, too.

Gift ideas for a pink or blue baby shower: the gift should have either of these colors to fit in with the theme. Suggestions include a baby book, diaper bag, rattle, crib blanket, crawler, playsuit, mittens, gown, receiving blanket, diapers, bathrobe, bottle holder, stuffed animal, rattle, crib bumper pads, tee shirts, carriage blanket.

Pin Shower

Everyone gets together, pools all money, and buys one large gift for the young mother. The idea here is that she probably has purchased plenty of smaller items such as booties or toys, and to give her smaller gifts would only duplicate what she already has. So one large item would be most welcome.

Invitations could be a white paper with a tiny gold pin in the corner and tell the guest that everyone is pooling resources for the large gift. This means you will receive the resources. You get together with all others and then you make the purchase.

Gift ideas for a pin shower: the single gift could be a high chair, crib, baby carriage, toy chest, stroller, bassinet, playpen, bottle warmer, baby scales, folding crib for traveling, vaporizer.

New Mama Shower

Because stork showers usually favor the baby, it could be a novelty to hold a shower for the new mama. Often, she has been so rushed with buying baby things, she has neglected her own needs. A few gifts for the mama will be very welcome, indeed. The invitation should be on pink note paper with bright blue ink. Emphasize the dainty and feminine since this fits in with the theme of the shower.

Gift ideas for a new mama shower: bed jacket, gown, plastic case for notions, perfumed soap, cosmetics, robe, small clock, slippers, lingerie, bed linens, cologne or fragrant toilet water, manicure set, hand mirror, monogrammed handkerchiefs, hosiery, robe, culottes.

Sewing Bee Shower

This calls for guests who love to sew and knit and want to make something very personal and individual for the guest-of-honor. Invitations could be miniature knitting needles, or an ordinary needle, stuck into a card with bits of yarn and cotton to give the effect. No decorations except covering the dining table with ribbons, lace, hot-iron transfers, sewing and knitting items, patterns. In advance, a small group decides what will be made for the little one. If the garment needs blocking as well as final touches to all the handwork, then an iron and ironing board should be brought along. If elaborate sewing or knitting plans are made, then the group should meet beforehand to decide upon the garment, pattern, correct size and color. *Note:* at a sewing bee shower, all invited guests bring the materials needed for the agreed-upon item and the gift is actually made right at the party. There are no packages to be opened, either. You should make the gift in advance or in the home of the hostess while the guest of honor just watches and chats with everyone.

Gift ideas for a sewing bee shower: mittens (knit or crochet), shawl, shirts, dress, gown, knit cap, sweater, booties, carriage cover, bibs, receiving blanket, kimono, pajamas, crawlers.

8.

The "Adopted Baby" Shower

The woman who adopts a child should also be given a baby shower, although there should be some slight modifications. These women will often show extreme gratitude at being showered for an adopted baby because they want to feel the joys of being feted for the event. For many such women, the baby shower will have a deeper meaning, perhaps, than for those who have borne their own children. It is perfectly within the realm of good taste to honor the mothers of these "chosen ones" with a shower for the adopted infant or young child.

As a hostess, you will derive a true sense of warmth and accomplishment for having made a woman feel like a real mother!

Invitations: It is advisable to write "for a chosen baby" on the outside of the invitation; include the name of the "chosen" child as well as the name of the mother who is to be the guest-of-honor. There is no reason why the baby cannot be present at the shower.

Decorations: Avoid using any reference to the stork for a shower party honoring a "chosen child." But you may use appropriate colors, pink or blue, as part of the basic color scheme. If the "chosen child" is somewhat older than a tiny infant, then use appropriate toys, scattered about in profusion, that are offered as gifts. Try a stuffed panda on top of a window sill, a Teddy bear on the hassock, a toy soldier on the piano. You might also have several dolls (for a girl) strewn about and if the child is old enough to crawl, urge her to scurry around and accumulate her own gifts.

Gift Ideas: plastic feeding apron, feeding dish, child's manicure set, sweater, slippers, toys of any kind for the proper age, crib mattress and crib sheets, wool shawl, pajamas, stuffed animal music box, training pants, pillowcases, gloves for an older child.

Entertainment: Have each invited guest bring along one of her own baby pictures. Shake all the pictures up in a small box, then ask the adoptive mother to try to correctly identify each baby with the guest mother at the party.

Refreshments: Keep it informal by serving angel food cake, ice cream or sherbet. Have a tray of cookies and small confections, together with lots of hot coffee, tea or punch.

9.

The Anniversary Shower

Every anniversary is a happy opportunity for a family-and-friend reunion and joyful reminiscences. Shower parties celebrated during the first ten or fifteen wedding anniversaries are usually informal gatherings. As the years increase, so does the dignity and significance of the observance. In planning an anniversary shower, here are two basic etiquette rules:

1. When the anniversary shower or party is given by the couple itself, no gifts are expected.

2. When the anniversary shower or party is given by friends and/or relatives, then gifts are permissible.

Tip: The shower may consist of individual gifts, one gift from the entire group, or just a shower of "good wishes" from all.

Wedding anniversaries should not pass unnoticed. They are joyful milestones in the lives of happily married people. It is thoughtful to hold a modest party or a more elaborate dinner shower, depending upon the mood, for the honored couple. Tradition has set up the theme for most anniversaries. They are given below, for easy reference and to help you in deciding the theme of the shower and appropriate gifts, if they are to be given.

WEDDING ANNIVERSARIES

First Year . . . . Paper
Second Year . . . . Cotton
Third Year . . . . Leather
Fourth Year . . . . Books and/or Fruits and Flowers
Fifth Year . . . . Wood
Sixth Year . . . . Iron
Seventh Year . . . . Wool and/or Copper
Eighth Year . . . . Bronze
Ninth Year . . . . Pottery
Tenth Year . . . . Tin and/or Aluminum
Eleventh Year . . . . Steel
Twelfth Year . . . . Linen and/or Silk
Thirteenth Year . . . . Lace
Fourteenth Year . . . . Ivory
Fifteenth Year . . . . Crystal
Twentieth Year . . . . China
Twenty-fifth Year . . . . Silver
Thirtieth Year . . . . Pearl
Thirty-fifth Year . . . . Coral and/or Jade
Fortieth Year . . . . Ruby
Forty-fifth Year . . . . Sapphire
Fiftieth Year . . . . Gold
Fifty-fifth Year . . . . Emerald
Sixtieth Year . . . . Diamond, yellow
Seventy-fifth Year . . . . Diamond Jubilee

Suggestions for an Anniversary Shower

The basic rules about holding a surprise party, inviting only those who are friends and/or relatives of the guests of honor, apply here. Of course, since an anniversary is a family affair, it is permissible for relatives to hold the party and to bestow gifts. If the anniversary couple should want to hold a celebration, invited friends and/or relatives need not bring gifts but the occasion is one of happy unity so those who wish to express their affection, may bring gifts to suit the theme of the occasion. Here are various suggestions:

First Anniversary: Paper

Decorate the house into a kaleidoscope of bright color. Use streamers of cellophane and confetti. Your invitations could be cards with glued-on colored confetti. Also, you could tear off a calendar page and mark the date with a red crayon and affix it to the invitation. Tables may be decorated with brightly colored paper covers and paper plates and napkins. Use paper forks and spoons and multi-colored straws for cold drinks. Serve buffet refreshments from a hard cardboard tray heaped with cellophane pompons of all bright rainbow colors. If these are attached to pencil stems, they can later be distributed as favors.

Gifts of Paper: plates, cups, saucers, spoons, napkins, tablecloths, towels, writing paper, exotic calendars, desk blotters, memo notebooks, engagement books, closet shelf accessories, stationery. *Tip:* present all gifts in a brown paper shopping bag that is decorated with paper streamers.

Second Anniversary: Cotton

Decorate the house with colorful little aprons cut out of bright prints. On small squares of cotton, ink-print your invitations and affix to small cards, suitable for mailing. At the shower party, cover a table with gay gingham or calico cotton print; in the center, have a row of small cotton plants made by attaching large puffs of cotton batting to natural or artificial plants. To add a realistic touch, use pods of dark-brown paper and raisin seeds. (Tattered brown, not green, leaves are natural when cotton is ripe.)

Gifts of Cotton: Aprons, handkerchiefs, kitchen towels, tablecloths, shoebags, napkins, pillow cases, quilts, bathmats, curtains, cotton laundrybag, bedding.

Third Anniversary: Leather

Decorate by using fringed leatherette material for the table and even the chair. A cute invitation could be the number 3 cut out in leather (gift shops and handicraft stores have such suitable leather) pasted onto a card. You might also paste cut-outs of leather garments onto the invitation. At the shower party, have a large leather wastebasket on the table in which all gifts are placed until overflowing. Excess gifts are placed around the leather wastebasket.

Gifts of Leather: House slippers, leather-covered picture frames, snapshot albums and leatherette desk accessories, purses, luggage, portfolios, briefcases, notebooks of all kinds (memo pads, address books, etc.) dresser sets, make-up kits, footstools, wardrobe boxes and shoes and footwear of any kind, provided you know proper sizes in advance.

Fourth Anniversary: Books and/or Fruits and Flowers

Use autumn foliage, real or artificial, to set the theme. Invitations could have real leaves pasted therein or use a diary page to signify a "book" theme. Decorate the room with various books as well as artificial fruits and flowers; then cover a

AUTUMN FOLIAGE

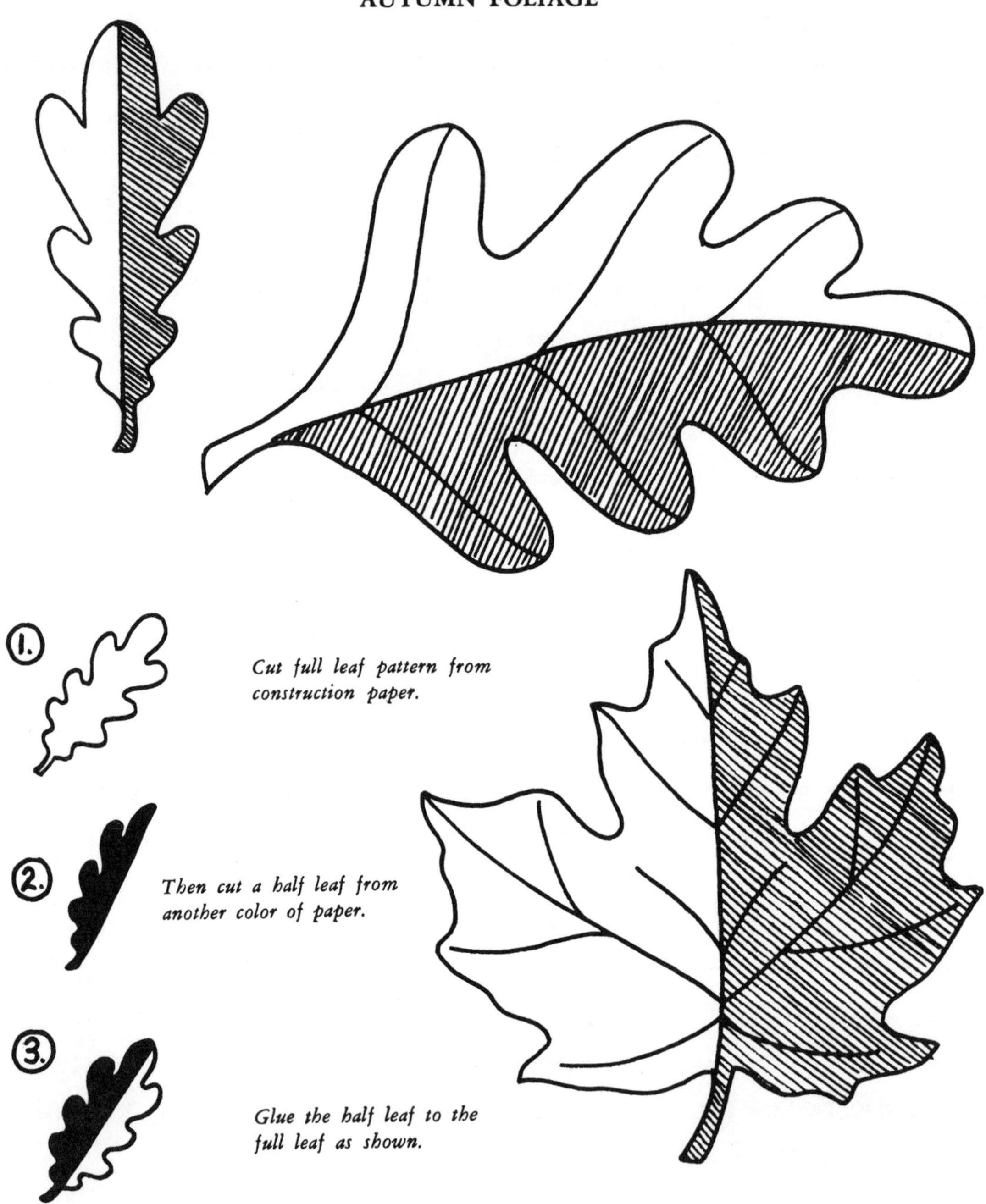

Draw the veins of leaf with a felt tip pen. Brown is ideal.

When making leaves, use yellow, orange, and brown construction papers.

table with a floral print. On top of the table, put huge bowls and fill with edible fruit. At this anniversary, everyone can eat the decorations!
Gifts of Books and/or fruits and flowers: Any popular book, sets of books, bookcases, magazines, magazine subscriptions, book plates, bookends, magazine racks. For edibles, any fresh fruit, baskets of fruit, dinnerware or wearing apparel with a fruit design. For flowers, include bulbs, seeds, plants, cuttings, shrubs, potted plants, gardening books, gardening equipment.

Fifth Anniversary: Wood

Send invitations on pine paper (available from most any wallpaper dealer) which is paper treated to resemble knotty pine. Write your invitation on this folded paper and emphasize the wooden theme. To decorate, use wooden bowls for flowers or fruits; if food is served, then provide each guest with a wooden tray, using wooden spoons and forks. Use a wooden chest, or even a painted barrel for presentation of gifts. The guests of honor may take the wooden chest, too.
Gifts of wood: Fireside woodbaskets, coffee tables, sewing tables, magazine racks, wooden salad services, footstools, bookends, wall plaques, wooden trays for all needs, ice buckets, pine pantry pails, door knockers, guest logs, candy boxes, cooky buckets, candlesticks and even a package of monogram-initialed pencils.

Sixth Anniversary: Iron

Small slivers or "shavings" of iron affixed to invitation cards help set the theme; use an iron colored card and paste on pictures of different iron objects. To decorate, have several iron kettles or jugs. If large enough gifts may be inserted within.

Gifts of iron: Pottery, cookware, tea service, stove accessories, cast iron utensils, knives, forks, spoons, Dutch oven, iron jewelry for a novelty. A sprinkle-steam pressing iron is one gift that says everything for an iron anniversary!

Seventh Anniversary: Wool and/or Copper

Invitations could contain bits of woolen yarn, or a copper colored motif, depending on the agreed-upon theme, or a combination of both. Decorate the room with woolen tablecloth, balls of wool in a copper basket make an excellent unison of both themes, and this is given as the gift, too.
Gifts of wool and/or copper: Blankets, small rugs of any size, depending upon the individual's budget, automobile robes, furlined slippers, wearing apparel. Copper pots and pans, copper cookware, waste baskets, desk sets trimmed with copper, canister set, breadbox.

Eighth Anniversary: Bronze

Use bronze colored invitations; paste pictures of bronze statues and bronze objects on the invitations. Decorate the room with bronze objects strewn around and a tablecloth that has a bronze color which might also be part of the gift giving.
Gifts of bronze: Kitchenware of any kind, pots and pans, waste baskets, cutlery sets, bronze colored sports items, bronze colored garments to wear, electric skillet, casserole cookware.

Ninth Anniversary: Pottery

From a South American travel agency, obtain picture folders showing pottery. Cut out the pots and paste on cards that have a pot shape. Use thick crayon to mark down the vital data. To

decorate, you might try a Mexican theme showing potted cactus, pottery donkeys and the lively colors of the peasant crafts.
Gifts of pottery: Stretch the imagination a bit. Use baskets, cookie bucket, ice bucket, ash trays, decanters, vases, statues, soup tureen set, drinking mugs, salad sets, spice rack, Lazy Susan set, peppermill set, salt and pepper shaker set, jugs. The emphasis is on a pottery design and this could also include clothing or towels or linens which have a Fiesta design, too.

Tenth Anniversary: Tin and/or Aluminum

Use tinfoil invitations that give a wonderful theme feeling. All gifts should be wrapped in tinfoil. Carry it further by having tinfoil-wrapped goodies, little cakes and candies, and serve on a tinfoil wrapped tray. Use a watering pot or metal wastebasket to hold gifts. *Note:* For this occasion, you may use any shiny white metal to convey the theme of tin.
Gifts of tin and/or aluminum: Picnic services, plates, cups, trays, kitchen cabinet accessories, pantry pails, garden watering buckets, seed cans and assorted gadgets ranging from an economical cookie cutter to a cookwear set, kitchenware, spun aluminum bowls, vases, goblets, breadtrays, percolators, teapots.

Eleventh Anniversary: Steel

Steel need not be cold in our modern age. Steel is available in such a variety of colors that it can be quite a cheerful occasion. Invitations may include a collage of steel housewares interspersed with cut out photos of steel mills (it is an interesting contrast). To add a dash to decorations, use a color scheme of black and silver with touches of green. Sharp geometric patterns help emphasize these colors to good advantage.

Gifts of steel: The "secret" here is to obtain objects of stainless steel. Use this for your guide. Suggestions include candlestick holders, knives, forks, spoons, sewing needles, silverplated coffee pot, silverplated round tray, small silverware chest, silverplated bon bon service, tea pot, sugar and creamer set, water pitcher, candelabra, butter dish, vegetable dish, bread tray, place settings, saucepan, skillet, Dutch oven, percolator, cake dish, double boiler, chicken fryer, canister, fry pan.

Twelfth Anniversary: Linen and/or Silk

Use any fabric to imprint the invitations; or, use fabric-edged invitation cards available in many boutiques. To decorate, take out some of your best linen and silk tablecloths, napkins and an apron, too. You might have a huge laundry bag to suggest the linen theme and in this, all gifts are given.
Gifts of linen:. Bedspread, sheets, pillowcases, tablecloths, napkins, aprons, handkerchiefs, comforter, set of placemats, dish towel set, kitchen towel set, bathroom towel set, sewing kit with material and pattern for a linen item that the guest of honor can use for making her own gift.

Thirteenth Anniversary: Lace

A lace-fringed handkerchief may be used for an invitation with washable words inscribed. To decorate, use lace trimmed tablecloth, have a lace-fringed curtain set, put out lace trimmed doilies upon which food is served in paper plates with a lace trim or a lace sketch.
Gifts of lace: Lingerie, clothing, gloves, slippers, handkerchiefs, towels, napkins, curtains, tablecloths, a bolt of lace trimmings, lace-trimmed handbags. *Tip:* Use a lace trimmed sack in which the gifts are placed. Later, the honoree takes the sack, as well.

Fourteenth Anniversary: Ivory

If available, use cutout photos of elephants with ivory tusks on sparkling white invitations. To decorate, use ivory-white candles for a setting. Buy toy elephants, carve them from soap or make them from marshmallows; use toothpicks with macaroni trunks and tails. Place cards may be cutout elephants and tiny imitation ivory novelties help add atmosphere.

Gifts of ivory: Emphasize the color of ivory to keep with the theme. Suggestions include ivory-white candles, ivory colored dinnerware, ivory-handled spoons, forks, knives, ivory colored statuettes, a miniature ivory elephant, ivory colored wearing apparel if you know the right size, an ivory colored photo album, ivory bracelet, ivory necklace and assorted pins and jewelry, ivory novelties from a boutique.

Fifteenth Anniversary: Crystal

Use cutout photos of crystal chandeliers and old-fashioned crystal glassware to be pasted on cellophane covered cards to emphasize the theme when sending invitations. To decorate, use as much crystal and glassware as possible. You might even use a mirror under the table centerpiece to reflect the beauty of a crystal bowl filled with glass flowers or edible fruit.

Gifts of crystal: Candlesticks, little blown-glass animals, small vials of perfume wrapped in cellophane, plates, glasses, dessert services, flower bowls, vases, powder and cosemetic jars, miscellaneous dressing table pieces, paper weights, small crystal lamps.

Twentieth Anniversary: China

For an invitation, use Oriental paper lanterns with a Chinese junk motif. Here's a cute tip: buy a Chinese newspaper, cut

ELEPHANT MOTIFS

The three elephant sketches shown are suggested for use as paper decorations or on invitations.

MARSHMALLOW ELEPHANT

Make this elephant with toothpicks, macaroni, and marshmallows.

ORIENTAL MOTIFS

out small sections and upon these, paste a small 3 x 5 card bearing all details as to time and place of the shower. To decorate, use lighted paper lanterns and long scrolls of red paper lettered in black and gold to duplicate Chinese characters. Use Chinese good luck charms, rice cake fortunes and incense to help carry out the theme. You may have ready-to-serve Chinese food for your guests. Visit a Chinese art shop for decoration ideas such as small wooden pagoda, a miniature rickshaw, floral patterns. Remember to use chopsticks as part of the decorative theme.

Gifts of china: candelabra, bowls, compote, vegetable dish, knives, forks, spoons, serving sets, sugar and creamer set, salt and pepper set, soup spoon, dinner fork, dinner knife, bread dish, celery dish, water pitcher, roll tray, plates, saucers, cups, goblets, stemware, punch bowl and cup set with ladle, crystal clarets, tinted tumbler set, tankard set, cocktail glasses, tea tumblers, ice water set, water pitcher.

Twenty-Fifth Anniversary: Silver

For invitations, use plain white informal notes which are lightly glued inside larger folders cut from silver paper. This is usually an important event and should have more elaborate decorations. A dinner would be in order for this special anniversary. A silver bowl is a lovely container which may have flowers, real fruit or other decorative beauty. A special cake may be made with an oak cluster which represents the family; one silvered leaf is included for each immediate relative and one silvered leaf with an acorn for the feted couple. You could use a silver bridal arch, an artificial frosted tree with little silver bells to improve the theme of the centerpiece. *Note:* Because silver gifts are usually costly, only the family and most intimate friends should participate in this gift shower.

Gifts of silver: sterling silver of any suitable need, candy dish, candlesticks, candelabra, salt and pepper set, hurricane lamps, vase, place setting, dinner plate, salad plate, bread and butter plate, jam and jelly set, sugar and creamer set, coffee pot, saucepan, skillet, double boiler, chicken fryer, percolator, cake dish, Dutch oven.

Thirtieth Anniversary: Pearl

Send invitations in the shape of a shell or a pearl; consider using cut out pictures of oysters and pearl beds of the oceans as a background. Decorations could include any shell-shaped pieces on a table covered with a cloth of tourquoise under white lace or lacepaper doilies to give the effect of sea foam. White or pink china and glassware is lovely. Try pink candles in white holders. Shell vases are good. Attach to each place card a part of a dime-store pearl necklace. Use seashell-shaped dishes to hold white mints. Emphasize the seashell shape. Present the gifts in a treasure chest draped with fish netting, crepe-paper seaweed and ropes of imitation pearls.

Gifts of pearls: Jewelry could include cameo pendant/pin with pearls, simulated cultured pearl set, pearl-studded aurora borealis pin set, cuff links and tie tac, jewel case with pearl jewelry, pearl necklace, manicure set with pearl handles, any houseware item with a pearl handle, pearl-colored radio, pearl-colored wearing apparel if you know the right size, pearl-colored curtains, pearl-colored dishes and clocks.

Thirty-Fifth Anniversary: Coral and/or Jade

This is a refreshing shower occasion; set the scene to suggest tropic seas. Invitations could have sketches of mermaids, seaweed, pirate chests, South Sea motifs. The decorations call for a tablecloth of pastel sea-green. Or—use a dyed fish net and

OCEAN MOTIFS

coral-colored accessories. If available, a lighted aquarium with bright fish splashing about helps create a refreshing salt-bitten atmosphere. Crepe paper fish adds more seagoing atmosphere.
Gifts of coral and/or jade: Fishing equipment to suggest the seas, gift of a vacation for two at a sea-splashed resort, coral colored tableware, jade jewelry ranging from necklace to cuff links, coral colored plates and dinnerware. Try obtaining wearing apparel in colors of coral and jade.

Fortieth Anniversary: Ruby

The emphasis here is upon the ruby color so use it in invitations as well as in decorations. Artificial rubies from a dime store as well as children's marbles with a ruby color also help set the scene. A ruby colored bowl to hold the gifts is suitable. Decorate the table with ruby glassware and gold-banded china on a contrasting creamy lace cloth. In the center, place a ruby colored bowl with some deep-red roses.
Gifts of rubies: Jewelry is appropriate and depends upon the individual budget. Select any glassware that has a ruby color. Cookware is now available in ruby colored enamel. For the economical, a ruby colored pair of curtains, tablecloth, place mats and napkin set, dinnerware in a ruby tint, glassware with a ruby tint, compact, lipstick, perfume in a ruby tinted atomizer.

Forty-Fifth Anniversary: Sapphire

The emphasis here is upon the sapphire color so you could use the motif in your invitations. Photo cutouts of the sapphire could be pasted upon the cards. Tradition holds that decorations include dark purple grapes or blue iris and delphinium for this anniversary shower. Cambridge blue glassware is particularly effective on a cloth of rose.

Gifts of sapphires: Jewelry, cutlery, clothing, luggage, sewing box, jewel case, combination vanity tray and dressing mirror, tissue box holder, cologne, French purse, billfold, French clutch purse, all with a sapphire color is much appreciated.

Fiftieth Anniversary: Gold

For this Golden Wedding Anniversary, a celebration should include a long guest list; for this reason, a tea or reception is wise. (For a smaller group, you could have a buffet luncheon or supper.) All friends should be included. The invitations may be written on snow white note paper, or on small white informal note paper enclosed in a larger folder of gold paper.

Decoration should be beautiful and the room should be filled with flowers: daffodils, yellow roses, chrysanthemums and any available golden blooms of the season. *Tip:* A centerpiece of yellow golden blooming roses in a ring bowl may be used to symbolize the ring of happiness for the couple. You might also use gold paper to transform all bowls and vases. To emphasize the golden theme, put a lace cloth over a foundation of gold or yellow satin. Cake plates should have gold lace-paper doilies and any candles on the cake should properly be gold. If plate favors are used, fasten a gold wedding band—from the dime store—to a small snow white card and, if possible, tie in an orange blossom or tiny rosebud. This card contains the original date of the wedding of the honored.

Gifts of gold: The color may be used in selecting gifts such as dinnerware sets, jewelry, clothing, sewing box, cologne in a gold colored atomizer, billfold, French clutch purse, chess or checker set, playing cards, golf clubs, umbrella, clothing (be sure to know correct size) or everyone may pool efforts and purchase a golden locket for the honored wife and a golden tie pin for the honored husband.

Fifty-Fifth Anniversary: Emerald

Use sea green colors in selecting invitation cards; write the information in green ink, use dime store emeralds to decorate the cards. The decorations emphasize the green color, with bowls of artificial fruits with the emerald color, as well as emerald-colored marbles in a greenish vase. Set the table with a cloth of very pale green and crystal glassware with amber or green color; use a bowl of translucent green grapes or ivy as the centerpiece.
Gifts of emeralds: Emphasize the color in properly sized robes, comforters, shawls, sweaters, socks, shoes, sewing kits, cushions, glassware, dinner sets, table napkins and tablecloth, curtains, draperies and rugs.

Sixtieth Anniversary: Diamond, Yellow

This is a rare occasion and deserves a distinguished celebration. Decorations should have subdued diamond color, with polished crystals and glimmering tableware. If possible, the guests should consist mostly of members of the family and very close friends. To decorate, set a lace cloth set with white and crystal. Burn white candles in diamond colored crystal holders.
Gifts of diamonds: It would be best to select several gifts that would be welcomed by these honored guests-of-honor. Perhaps a diamond wristwatch, or a diamond brooch as well as a diamond tiepin for the husband. Since these are elderly people, the anniversary shower should be kept within good taste; the couple should not be surrounded with excitement or confused by large numbers of people. Invitations might best be made either by telephone or by using snow white cards and off-white inked messages.

Seventy-Fifth Anniversary: Diamond Jubilee

Follow same pattern as for the 60th anniversary, but do bear in mind the advanced age of the honored couple, and do not tire them with too many guests or presentations of gifts. Often, a hand-made diamond-designed shawl for the wife and a diamond pocket watch for the husband is sufficient. At this distinguished age, there is less of a material emphasis upon gifts and the honored couple will feel that being showered is a gift enough, along with the gift of having enjoyed 75 years of happiness and joy.

Summary: A wedding anniversary shower is a most personal and intimate kind of entertaining, whether you are giving the shower for another couple or even celebrating your own anniversary. In some situations, the rules of etiquette could be stretched and the couple may call for a shower. Always, the guest list should include available members of the original wedding party, family and friends. Keep in mind the *theme* of the anniversary and guide your shower accordingly so you will have a memorable and happy experience.

The menu for a wedding anniversary shower depends on the kind of party you are giving for the couple, whether buffet or dinner. But every party celebrating a wedding should really include a beautiful cake in facsimile of the original wedding cake, complete with bride and groom figurines. The cake should be the centerpiece in a buffet-supper table, or can be the climax at the end of a dinner party.

As a further gesture to the original wedding celebration, each guest can be given a piece of cake to take home, in a small box, tied with ribbon.

10.
The Office Shower

There are times when you will want to combine business with a party; for example, you may want to shower the event of a fellow worker who has become engaged, or promoted. To help keep the surprise, come into the office about an hour earlier and prepare all decorations. If it is to be a very brief shower, then do it during your lunch hour. At the last minute, have the guest of honor called away from the desk so that decorations and gifts can be arranged.

When to Hold an Office Shower

It is suitable to hold an afternoon shower for a worker who is being moved or transferred to a different branch of the company in a different city, or to another plant in the same region. Use the lunch hour for new promotion parties. If it is to honor a special worker such as an executive and you want to have more of a celebration, hold it in the very early evening.

New Promotion Parties

This kind of shower party is usually given by business associates in the place of business. The time of the shower party can be during the lunch hour, afternoon coffee break, or at the end of the business day. A small committee should plan this party (word of mouth is okay and no printed invitations are needed), without the guest of honor knowing about it. Try to surprise him or her.

Choose a place where everyone can sit around and chat and spend some time talking about the new duties. A gift purchased through contributions of those attending the party is nice and *should relate to the job.*

Decorations: Cover the desk with a huge business graph, or cut out pages from the newspaper with a business section dominating the scene. Use transparent tape to secure to the desk. *Caution:* No matter how informal an office you work in, it is a place of business! Streamers and balloons are in bad taste and might easily be taboo! *Alternate:* A few easily-whisked-out-of-sight ornaments might embellish the desk or table upon which gifts are arranged; but these should be set up and removed at a moment's notice. *Guideline:* "Business, as well as show business, must go on!"

Gift Ideas: mechanical pencil, desk pad and blotter, ruler, memo pad, watch band, pen and pencil holder, small desk picture frame, small bookcase, stamp holder, initialed key chain, desk or travel alarm clock, personalized stationery, framed auto or hunting prints, book ends, pen and pencil set, briefcases, desk barometer combination, bulletin board, desk caddy, telephone index, land and sea globe, perpetual calendar, butane lighter, dictionary, magnifier glass, stapler kit, pocket watch.

Refreshments: Keep this at a minimum because this is taking place in the office which is a place of business. A box of candy passed around is always suitable, or have ice cream brought in, coffee or punch served in gaily colored paper cups, small sandwiches, or a cake that is cut up and served with a beverage. Use a buffet service for refreshments. *Note:* Always ask your employer's permission for planning a shower party and, if suitable, invite him, too. If he is the honored guest, ask his superior. Do not serve alcoholic beverages of any sort at an office party.

Business Anniversary Shower Parties

These business anniversary shower parties are given for anyone who has had a successful career for a certain period of time with the company. Usually, such an anniversary shower is for accomplishment and could be as short as one year, if his or her accomplishment has been great, or for a given period such as a tenth anniversary or longer.

An anniversary shower party can be given by the owner of a company for an employee. Or, employees can give the shower party for the boss as recognition for the success of the company and how they all worked together as a team.

Feature a cake with the appropriate definition of the time-honored person inscribed on it; that is, whether he is a clerk, a salesman, a manager, an engineer, etc. This gives it a personal touch. At business anniversary shower parties, guests are those directly involved with the company, office or individual. No printed invitations are necessary, just word of mouth.

While the anniversary itself cannot be a secret, the party can be a surprise and should be given when it does not interfere with business. Arrangements can be as vast as time allows and food should be served to suit the occasion. *Suggestion:* Call a local caterer and tell him how many guests you will be having and ask for his services to accommodate this particular party. He can probably arrange box lunches or a buffet service for everyone.

Gift Ideas: While the office theme could be maintained, you could use something more personal. Suggestions include transistor radio, favorite records or record album, tickets to a local show, an all-expenses-paid weekend for two at a resort, electric shaver, wallet, purse, key case, inexpensive instamatic camera, telescope, thermos bottle set, picnic jug, hand carved wooden figurines, soap-on-a-rope, cologne, pen-and-pencil set, desk barometer, travel alarm clock, embossed brass wall plaque, stack stools, ash tray, electric thermos, thermometer.

Added tip: If time is valuable, considering that you are holding this shower party during office hours, you might pool all your money together and purchase one or two gifts at the most. This saves time in opening gifts and also shows that everyone got together for the occasion for this one "giant" gift.

11.

The Housewarming Shower

A housewarming party is usually given by a couple who has just moved into a new house or apartment; or it can be given for them (as a surprise) by their friends. But for this particular shower, it is best to let the couple hold the party themselves. What about being surprised by friends? This is unwise since you may catch them at their worst and when they are embarrassed and unprepared.

Such a shower includes friends and relatives, too.

Decorations: The best decorations would be to have clean and attractive rooms to show off to all the guests. Since they have ooohed and ahhed as they walk around the home, it is wise to have everything arranged neatly and in good taste. *Optional:* streamers, gaily colored ribbons attached to a small box that is cut in the shape of a house. Into this cardboard house, all gifts are placed as guests enter. These gifts are to be opened later on.

Invitations: Black construction paper cut into the shape of a door mat. Write WELCOME in white ink across the center. Ordinarily, when people give their own housewarming parties, they do not designate them as such; that would be too much like asking for contributions. It is best to call it "Open House" which is self-explanatory.

Refreshments: A buffet is suitable. You might try to serve fruit punch and cupcakes. Or, on a table, place a large punch bowl, and surround it with plates of small sandwiches, snacks, nuts, fruit slices, cookies, cakes, dainties, and let guests serve themselves.

Gifts: The idea of one big gift is a good one since this makes it less "commercial" because the couple arranged this "Open House" event. Suggested gifts include: door mat, wall can opener, iron, shower curtain, bed lamp, electric fan, demitasse cup and saucers, ironing board, snack tables, clothes hamper and matching waste basket, recipe-filing box, assorted brooms, picnic basket complete with thermos, cups and saucers and cutlery, travel kit, matching luggage sets, matching clutch purse and men's wallet set, assorted soaps for personal and laundry use, sets of "his and hers" bath towels, kitchen towels.

Suggestion: Occasionally, when a young couple is starting out with a very limited budget, their families and close friends give a shower party for them in order to help furnish their home. Sometimes, too, an elderly couple, whose children have married, will start housekeeping in a small apartment once again. In this case, the children may want to give them a shower. Naturally, such a shower is held in the evening and both men and women are present. The gifts are the same as those for a bride-to-be. Refreshments should be very simple buffet style.

12.

The "Going Away on a Trip" Shower

You can share the thrill of a friend's planned trip by giving her a travel or Bon Voyage shower. A shower of small gifts and many good wishes is a wonderful way to help a friend go off on a well-deserved trip. The honored guest will be in a festive mood with a vacation on her mind and the shower helps add to the joyous built-in atmosphere.

Suggestion: The theme of this shower party depends upon the type of trip to be made—whether by boat, train, plane, car or bus, and also the destination. Plan your shower party with these facts in mind.

Invitations: Picture post cards make ideal invitations for a '"Going Away On A Trip" shower. You might obtain scenic views of the place where she will be vacationing. Or, cut out squares of a road map and use a thick red crayon to mark down the details of the invitation. Insert these road map squares in an envelope and adorn with some travel stickers to give a proper mood to the occasion.

Decorations: Maps make very colorful decorations. You may also use travel folders, picture post cards, tour advertisements, train schedules. Paste ordinary maps on cheesecloth or muslin and shellack them when the paste is thoroughly dry. *Note:* keep method of transportation in mind. A bus schedule

GOING AWAY SHOWER MOTIFS

His and Her invitation patterns. Draw figures with felt tip pen.

would be inappropriate for someone travelling by ship. Decorate a table with a child's railroad station toy set that looks surprisingly "travel-ish." Place gifts all around the railroad station or toy town or any available decoration. You might also have a large battered suitcase to store the gifts and then have the guest-of-honor open it up at the proper moment.

Gift ideas: luggage identification tags, travel diary, camera and case, travel iron, overnight case, permanent press garments, cologne, scarf, wallet, umbrella, travel manicure set, billfold, utility set, pocket secretary with pen, money clip, key case, cigarette case, electric shaver, tote bag, supply of film (if you know the camera), travel stationery set.

Refreshments: It would be best to keep it simple and very informal. A buffet with sandwiches and lots of hot coffee, tea or punch is usually sufficient.

Shower for a Ship Mate

If your honor guest is to make a boat voyage, you could send out announcement cards shaped like a life saver. Attach candy Life Savers to complete the effect. A bit of ribbon, about four inches long, is run through the hole in the candy; then the double ribbon is threaded through a series of small slits in the card. Use contrasting color of ribbon to that of the card. *Example:* if your card is light pink, your Life Saver should be tied with bright blue ribbon.

An attractive table centerpiece could be a small ship mounted on a mirror reflector. Paper anchors could serve as place cards. Fish nets also help create a decorative mood.

Gifts could be wrapped in fish nets to help establish a related theme to travelling by ship.

Riding the Rails Shower

If your honor guest is going by railroad, your invitations could contain railroad tracks as a design, a railroad time table upon which the information is printed with thick black crayon. Decorations may consist of toy trains and a toy track. An attractive table centerpiece could be a small toy train on a track that is strewn with the various gifts. The object is to remove the gifts so the railroad can continue. Wrap gifts in timetable paper.

"Fly Through the Air" Shower

If your honor guest is going by airplane, your invitations could contain pasted cut outs of different airplanes, airports, pilots. Decorations could consist of a large toy airplane surrounded by various gifts. You could wrap gifts in an airplane time schedule.

The Auto Shower

If your honor guest is going by auto, then your invitations could contain pasted cut outs of gasoline and auto supply advertisements. A road map is also suitable for such a trip. On cut out segments of a road map, write down the data of the invitation. Decorations could be miniature automobiles on a large table covered with a road map. Gifts are included on this table. Gifts, too, may be wrapped in the maps.

The Bus Trip Shower

Follow the same pattern as for the auto shower, but you might also include pasted photos of different types of buses. *Suggestion:* use photos of antique buses to help set the mood.

Gifts are wrapped in road maps and placed upon a table that is covered with another map.

Follow the Theme Guideline in Selecting Appropriate Gifts

If the honor guest is to go to a warm climate, the gifts should be those she could use during her stay in the tropics. If she is to go to a cold climate, select appropriate gifts for that occasion. Or, if it is to be a ship's voyage where all her needs will be taken care of, then she will welcome clothing and personal items. You will have a shower success for the vacationer if you select decorations and gifts to fit in with the ultimate destination and the theme of the trip.

Always welcome: An assortment of film for a camera, luggage, personal items such as cosmetics, cologne, soaps, toiletries, books and magazines, guide books, maps of the ultimate destination, socks, slippers, etc.

13.

The "Off to School" Shower

The "off to school" shower is rather pre-planned and works out quite well. The guests are probably about the same age since the school-bound youngster will want his close friends at the shower. This makes it easy to plan a shower as far as gifts, recreation and refreshments are concerned. Furthermore, these young people do have a common interest and such a shower is sure to be filled with lots of fun.

Invitations: Shape doubled construction paper into a college pennant; select the appropriate school colors that the student will be supporting for the coming season. If time permits, write to the school and ask if they have small stickers with the school's seal to paste on a pennant that they have available. Use these for the invitation. Or, try a diploma scroll upon which you handwrite the details of time and place.

Decorations: Young folks will like enormous panda bears or large stuffed animals—perhaps a skunk, a tiger, a dog or a cat—you might learn the school mascot and then obtain an appropriate stuffed animal. Plaster pennants on the walls. If you want to add some conversational controversy, obtain pennants of rival schools. You could pin dance programs, party invitations, college beanies to a special bulletin board. Beneath, could be a table containing gifts. Use streamers of crepe paper in the school colors, twisted from a central ceiling fixture and draped to all four corners to make the room more "schoolishly" party minded.

To keep a collegiate atmosphere from becoming too heavily academic, disperse books, horn-rimmed spectacles, mortarboard caps, rolled diplomas, about the room.

Tip: Make an inverted mortarboard cap by attaching a square of cardboard to the bottom of a paper cup and coloring the whole thing black. Add a paper fringe tassel in the school colors.

For place cards, make miniature books by pasting a mat stock "binding" over one edge and two broad sides of the little booklike boxes in which paper clips are sold. Let the "binding" extend one inch beyond the white pages. On the front cover, hand letter the name of the guest.

Gift ideas: Let your decision be guided by the status of the student. Example: beginning students will welcome snack sets, pajamas, book ends, laundry bags, snapshot albums. Advanced or graduate students will like personal jewelry, a new fountain pen, books that will help him in his trade or profession, a camera.

Other gift ideas include: pen-and-pencil set, notebooks, monogrammed stationery with pre-stamped envelopes, alarm clock, scrapbook, bracelet with engraved name, electric shaver, stadium boots, zipper looseleaf book, shoe bag, hotplate, bathrobe, slippers, luggage, socks, loafers, trunk, calendar, combination lock, umbrella, key case, wallet, billfold, belt, utility kit, money clip, manicure case, soap-on-a-rope, desk stapler, intensity folding lamp, any special supplies he will need in schoolwork.

Refreshments: Keep it informal. A buffet is good, which may include sandwiches, potato chips, lots of soft drinks, a punch bowl, small cakes, cookies, some confections.

14.

The "Special Holiday" Shower

You can turn a traditional holiday into a party shower by following the basic principles outlined in this volume. A shower party is a fun-filled occasion that calls for the exchange of gifts to honor a special person. When you stretch this idea, you can hold a shower party to honor a special occasion. You may single out one person who is to be the guest of honor and hold the party in her favor. The *theme* of the party determines how you will celebrate. The guest of honor receives the various gifts, as always. These need not be costly because the occasion is a traditional holiday and not too personal as with other showers outlined in this volume. But they can provide much joy for all the party guests and the guest of honor and help strengthen the bonds of friendship. Here are various holidays and how you can use them to create a shower party.

New Year's Eve Shower

Invitations could be upon calendar pages of the new year. Try standard greeting cards available in most dime stores, boutiques and gift shops. Bells of all sizes are suitable decorations. Hang them from the ceiling; arrange flat bells in an effective frieze over the fireplace or on the buffet table. Use silver, gold, red, white, blue or any color that blends with the rest of your plans. For this shower party, present gifts before mealtime. Gifts may be any inexpensive gadgets.

Valentine's Day Shower

Use a valentine for an invitation. Try a quaint, lacy, old-fashioned one upon which you write the invitation. Make your own out of cellophane paper that has a red tinge, and paste it on stiff white paper. Decorative color scheme should be red and white throughout; use red hearts, arrows, Cupids, dangling on red strings or ribbons from doorways. Refreshments should be buffet style. Cover the table with a white cloth, sprinkled with red hearts and centered with a low white bowl surrounded by red hearts and filled with red flowers. *Tip:* An economical centerpiece may be made from four large red cardboard hearts that have been secured at the corners to make a square container. Fill it with white flowers or use it for receiving gifts. If you have white napkins, attach gummed hearts to the corners. Refreshments carry the same red-white theme. A white cake with a red heart is always welcome. You might try beet and cauliflower salad, white cottage cheese sprinkled with paprika, heart-shaped sandwiches, a red gelatin salad that has been molded in individual or large heart-shaped molds, heart-shaped cookies sprinkled with red sugar or dotted with candied cherries. Lots of hot coffee. Or, you could have lots of red punch in a white bowl! Shower gifts should be small items such as handkerchiefs, little jewelry things, gifts of stationery with a red heart as an imprint.

St. Patrick's Day Shower

March 17th is the day that the Irish came into their own.

You don't have to be Irish to hold a shower party for St. Patrick's Day. It's a perfect time to get together and have lots of fun. An invitation could be sent out using dime store or gift shop greeting cards for St. Patrick's Day. Or make your own by tracing an Irish top hat on green construction paper with black ink. Or cut shamrocks from green mat stock and write invitations down in white ink and mail in green-stamped envelopes. To decorate, try to have shamrocks, clay pipes, potatoes, lots of green ribbons and the familiar Irish top hat, all over the celebration room. As a novelty, obtain a sack of large-sized Irish potatoes. Scrub potatoes well. Cut a hole through the center, run green ribbons through and string together, or use as individual "place cards." Later, the scrubbed potatoes can be boiled and eaten. Refreshments could be the aforementioned Irish potatoes, corned beef and cabbage, Irish coffee, a green-iced cake with an Irish flag floating on top. *Tip:* serve the meal on a table covered with green cellophane over which a lace cloth has been placed. It makes an interesting and appropriate effect. Napkins could have the harp, pipe and shamrock designs. These are available at most gift shops. Keep gifts simple such as green jewelry, green wearing apparel, a green book cover, a green pen and pencil set, a green desk diary, a green scarf or a record album containing Irish songs.

Spring Shower

Greet the arrival of Spring with an invitation made out of a simple correspondence card, sporting a bright umbrella, suggesting the familiar April shower. Or use a floral covered card to symbolize the approaching green season of flowers in bloom. Keep decorations simple and cheerful. A few vases of fresh flowers help establish the mood. To emphasize the April shower theme, have a cloth umbrella covered in pink or green paper ruffles with the handle wrapped in ribbon. Gifts may be placed underneath the umbrella which is suspended from a floral colored streamer attached to the ceiling or to the wall. *Or:* a bright colored umbrella is the one gift given to the guest of honor. Refreshments are buffet style with simple sandwiches, salad, a loaf cake, lots of coffee and tea and punch.

Maytime Shower

This calls for a floral setting; the invitations are decorated with multi-colored flowers and blossoms. The house is decorated with lots of flowers; a "must" is arranging blossoms in a green or patterned vase which is put on the table. A tablecloth should have floral patterns that may match the napkins and place mats. Use spring flowers throughout. Refreshments call for simple items such as paper-thin sandwiches, wafers, mints, a gelatin salad molded in flower shapes, lots of beverages. Gifts could be surprisingly inexpensive and appropriate such as: a packet of flower seeds, a garden plant, a vase, a gardening book, some cuttings from flowers, herb seeds and a bouquet of flowers.

Fourth of July Shower

Emphasize the traditional American colors of red-white-blue in your invitations. You might paste flag stickers on white cards, or obtain stickers of Uncle Sam to be used on small papers. Even ordinary stars would be suitable to create the mood. Decorate the room with red-white-blue streamers, paper flags, paper plates with the same colors. Obtain balloons of individual red, white, blue colors and tie them in proper order around the table. For a centerpiece on the table, use an Uncle Sam doll. Refreshments continue the mood. Red jelly in white

HALLOWEEN MOTIFS

These familiar halloween motifs may be used on invitations or as paper decorations.

Cut Bats from black construction paper. Fasten to drapes, tablecloth, etc. with a double-stick cellophane tape. Fold large bat in half and use as invitation. Simply glue a piece of white paper inside to write message on.

and blue dishes, spread on thin white crackers. Ice cream in a fancy mold, or vanilla ice cream with crushed strawberries over the top. Plain white cakes that have been iced in red and blue may accompany the ice cream. Red punch in a blue bowl served in white cups is ideal. Gifts should be very simple such as neckties, kerchiefs, hand towels, all in the red-white-blue colors or as close as possible.

Autumn Shower

This is your Indian Summer shower which can include a circus motif, also. Invitations could be cut outs of teepees, or cut out pictures of late summer, bow and arrow, the buffalo grazing in the fading sunset. Decorations emphasize the changing of the seasons such as popular paintings showing this time of the year, or Indians in their tents, riding horseback. Refreshments may include barbecued frankfurters, roasted corn, apple pie, lots of punch. Gifts should be very simple and may include cosmetic kits, towel sets, gift certificates to a local shop, transistor radio.

Halloween Shower

Youngsters love Halloween because it calls for dressing up in masquerade. There are no age limits for a Halloween shower. Invitations should have sketches of a black cat, a flying witch, a grinning jack o' lantern. *Tip:* On a folder of black construction paper, paste a dark gray cat cut-out. Make it realistic by pasting on cat whiskers made of ordinary sewing thread. Or, invitations are shaped like a grinning pumpkin. Many are available at dime store and gift shops. The decorations in the room should call for cardboard jack o' lanterns, orange crepe paper, paper cornstalks, grinning pumpkins, lots of witches on

THANKSGIVING MOTIFS

The familiar Thanksgiving motifs shown on this page may be used on invitations or as paper decorations.

broomsticks, all strewn about. Refreshments call for a simple buffet with sandwiches and beverages. Paper plates should carry the same Halloween theme. Gifts should be very simple and may include games, a book of spooky ghost stories, an eerie record or tape, a collage of cutout pictures of witches and ghosts to make up a framed picture.

Thanksgiving Shower

In honor of the Pilgrims who first designated November as a time of Thanksgiving, use a Pilgrim hat as an invitation. Use a light gray or white paper upon which is drawn a black hat with a silver buckle. The entire design may be traced with a crayon; or, cut a hat from black patent-leather paper and paste on a piece of paper. You might also use turkey pictures on the invitation—but if you do this, then you should serve turkey to your guests. Decorations call for the Pilgrim motif, using the traditional high hat, the turkey, pumpkin, even a replica of the Mayflower. Gift shops have paper fun things that can turn an ordinary table into a festive mood. Refreshments should include turkey sandwiches, cranberry sauce, pumpkin pie and lots of hot punch. Gifts should be very simple such as cutlery, flatware, dishes, cooking pots.

Christmas Shower

Invitations call for traditional Christmas cards available at all gift shops. You can make your own—take shiny red patent-leather paper. Stick a tinsel star on the top, using rubber cement. Write the invitation on the bottom and give specific details. Decorations at home call for a Christmas tree, or a wreath, toy snowballs, white darning or crochet cotton shaped like a snowball, Christmas-tree balls and ornaments, sprays of

CHRISTMAS MOTIFS

cedar or pine, mistletoe, red candles, a collection of Christmas cards. Refreshments should include roast turkey, cranberry sauce, red gelatin shaped like a star, Christmas cookies, spiced candied sweet potatoes, fruit cake, coffee. Gifts call for anything ranging from a box of home-baked gingerbread men to a television set! This is a festive time of the year and gift giving goes all the way, so be prepared for it.

A Ranch Shower

Do you love Western movies? Are you thrilled by watching far horizons, long days in the sagebrush and firelit evenings filled with cowboy singing? Then enjoy a Ranch Shower in the spirit of traditional western hospitality. It could be held any time during the year, but warm weather seems to be more favorable to the mood of the great outdoors. Send rodeo handbill invitations. To decorate, use lots of toy cowboys, horses, Indians. You might cover a table with a Navajo blanket, have a few Mexican sombreros strewn about. Add vivid posters or magazine covers showing western scenes. *Tip:* Instead of napkins, use gala bandanna neckerchief cloths, squares of bright cotton prints, red, blue or yellow. Try to obtain a lantern and eat by this light. If possible, try to hold it outdoors. A backyard barbecue pit gives you the free spirit of the West and an authentic atmosphere, Refreshments could be barbecued meat, barbecue sauce, steak sandwiches, scrambled eggs with chipped beef, hot biscuits, pie or doughnuts and strong coffee. *Suggestion:* When it's time to eat, hammer on an old iron triangle and yell, "Come and get it!" If no iron triangle available, try a metal hoop or tin bucket. Hit it hard and fast to get that traditional Western triple beat that a ranch cook achieves by hitting the three sides of his triangle in rapid succession. Gifts may be leather items such as slippers, jackets, shoes, boots (but

Ranch Shower invitation pattern.

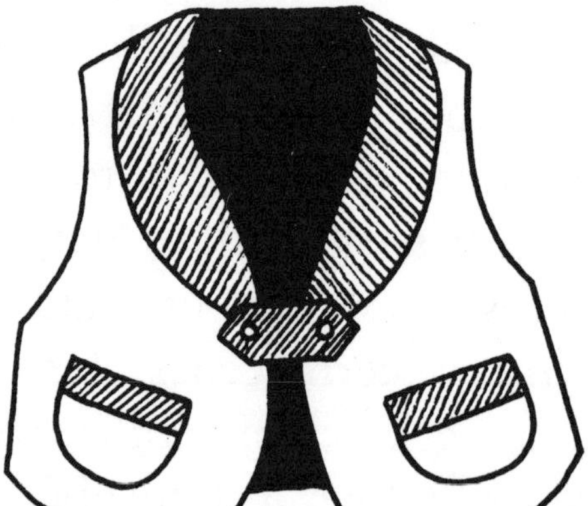

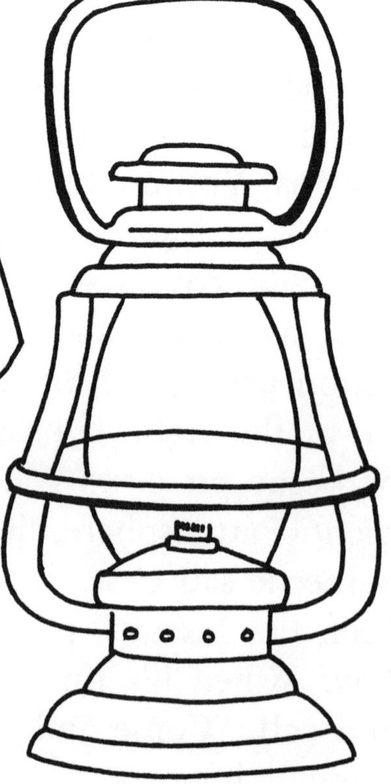

know the proper size in advance), leather figurines, leather bookends, novelty leather lamps and anything with a Western motif. An Indian blanket is always welcome and fits right in the mood!

Additional Suggestions

Carry the same themes for other occasions including Mother's Day, Father's Day, changing of the seasons, Treasure Hunt, Circus Time, Going Away Shower, Coming Home Shower, Get Well Shower (when person comes home and is capable of being feted,) Promotion Party (to fete the person who was promoted in the office, to be held at home by friends and neighbors) or any situation that calls for a happy fun-filled celebration and giving of gifts.

New Clergyman Shower

In some rural sections, the minister's salary is very small and a shower is arranged to help furnish the rectory. This type of shower might be held in the parish house in the evening and the men of the congregation should be urged to cooperate. Decorations and selection of gifts are determined by the particular denomination and the local customs. Get together with the members of the particular church and decide upon appropriate decorations, refreshments and gifts that would be in keeping within the bounds of good taste.

A shower should be filled with fun. No matter what the occasion, a shower should be filled with fun and joy. It is a splendid opportunity for bringing together friends and relatives and sharing of experiences and gifts. It is a memorable experience and should be part of your quest and pursuit of happiness.

15.

Twenty-five Ideas for Special Showers

Because there has to be a built-in reason for holding a shower party, it is essential to pick a theme and carry it through from the start to the finish. Often, you will want to hold a shower party because it is fun-filled and something "different" from a stereotyped party. You may select a theme and get together with friends, select an honoree, and then follow the basic principles outlined in the first four chapters of this volume. In so doing, you will have a successfully happy shower party. Here is a list of 25 different ideas for special showers.

1. Herbal Shower

Fill the honored guest's spice rack or spice chest with necessary and exotic herbs and spices. Everyone brings a different herb or spice.

2. Gadget Shower

Gather basic and fun-to-have household gadgets. You might put a $1.00 limit on the gift, so it need not be too costly. Gadgets for the entire house are appropriate for this shower.

3. Disposables Shower

Seek out the latest in pretty paper plates, cups, napkins, coasters, paper dresses and party aprons. If it is a disposable, bring it along as a gift.

4. Scrub-a-Dub Shower

Make the guest of honor enjoy her dishwashing by feting her with an assortment of colorful dishcloths, towels, sponges and other dishwashing aids.

5. Fabulous Plastics Shower

Bring the latest in handsome stacking containers, drainage board, storage aids, glasses and dishes made of plastic.

6. Candlelight Shower

Select long candles, short candles, fat candles, skinny candles and off-beat candles. You will, naturally, decorate by having candlelight in the party room.

7. Christmas Beauties Shower

Stage this shower at Christmas time when ornaments are available. Gifts consist of such ornaments exclusively.

8. Closet Needs Shower

Turn a mundane closet into a fashion room with accessories such as padded hangers, clothing and blanket cases, racks for shoes, tie racks, skirt racks, and cases to serve all closet needs.

9. Witch's Fare Shower

Found up an assortment of all the brooms and brushes needed to clean house from top to bottom. (*Note:* you present the gifts, but are not asked to pitch in and do the housecleaning!)

10. Sewing Notions Shower

Outfit a sewing box with needles, pins, pin cushion, thread, snaps, hooks, scissors and other notions.

11. Pressing Paraphernalia Shower

Include a colorful dust cover and pad for the ironing board, sprinkling can or bottle, a press cloth, a tailor's ham and cans of spray starch and fabric finish.

12. Party Supply Shower

Give everything from cans of gourmet treats to serving trays, confetti, streamers, cocktail napkins and coasters.

13. Wooden Ware Shower

Consider wooden spoons and cutting boards, bowls, boxes and trays, along with a rolling pin and mortar and pestle, even boxes of pencils.

14. Measurings Shower

Make a collection of household measuring cups and spoons, a tape measure, yardstick and an assortment of rulers.

15. Horticultural Odds and Ends Shower

Supply the guest of honor with flower frogs and florist's putty, bowls, vases, pots and a sprinkling can and seeds, as well.

16. Hodge-Podge Shower

Put a $2.00 limit on the gift and give anything and everything. *Who says that a shower has to be expensive?*

17. Shipwreck Discotheque Shower

While a friendly native spins the discs, make merry in an island setting. Gifts fit in with needs for a shipwreck.

18. Endless Summer Safari Shower

Hang ten at a surfers' party decked with surfboards and rolling blue murals or, better yet, make it a beach or pool-side party in which guests bring all surfing-related gifts from an expensive board to a bottle of suntan lotion!

19. Olympic Meet Shower

Call it a come-as-your-favorite-sportsman shower party. Decorate with a variety of sports equipment, headlines and pictures. Everyone brings a sports gift from a golf ball to a boxed game or golf clubs.

20. Highland Fling Shower

Ask "clans" to vie in Scottish-style entertainment and costumes. Serve shortbread and usher in each "clan" to the drone of bagpipes from a record or tape or the real thing. Gifts call for anything that is Scot-related.

21. Computer Blast Shower

To celebrate the age of cybernetics, punch out invitations on computer cards (if available) and add a code number for each man with a corresponding one given to a girl. Instruct each to find his computer mate. Build a machine of aluminum foil, light bulbs, radio and car parts, etc., with a "voice" to give the wrong answers. Gifts fit in with the age of the computer.

22. Ancient Greek Revival Shower

Make it an evening with the gods of Olympus in which everyone masquerades as a mythological personality. Serve nectar and for games, feature mock discus (paper plate) and javelin (feather) throws. Gifts fit in with the Grecian theme.

23. Carnaby Street Super Shower

Here's a chance to wear your most "mod" of mad, mad outfits and to try out British accents, both high and low. Play the latest recorded hits imported from Britain. Gift giving includes anything that is made in Great Britain.

24. Sadie Hawkins Hoedown Shower

In a turnabout, ask the lady folk to invite their favorite boys to a jamboree. Bring guitars, fiddles, auto harps, washtub basses and musical saws and trade ballads of America's hill country; yodelers also welcome. Gifts reflect mountain folk ranging from checkered ginghams to traditional recipes.

25. Celebrity Gala Shower

Make it an "important and beautiful people" shower with disguises, large hats, enormous, brilliantly dyed sunglasses. Each "celebrity" imitates the character represented. Gifts could include anything that smacks of Hollywood and Broadway and that includes tickets to a show, old fan magazines, photos of famous folks, even a camera if the budget permits.

A Pot-Pourri of Different Shower Ideas

You may have recipe showers in which the gift consists of a favorite or family secret recipe; try a Gay Nineties shower in which everyone celebrates the good old days with gifts of appropriate clothing or records of those bygone days; the Roaring 20's symbolizes the days of bathroom gin so serve simulated gin and present a bottle of "moonshine" as a gift from a speakeasy friend; old movies shower calls for showing different old movies and looking over old fan magazines with gifts of tickets to a local art theatre showing film revivals; a book shower calls for filling up a bookshelf which may also be given along with the books; a rent money shower is delicate because it calls for money, so observe all etiquette rules; a golden West shower reflects the wide open spaces and a gift of a cactus plant or leather ranch boots would fit right in; a Spanish shower with posters of Spain is romantic as well as clothing and jewelry of a Latin style; a Hawaiian shower calls for wearing the styles of the islands and drinking fresh fruit juice and giving a gift of a pineapple or gaily imprinted clothing; a reunion shower calls for old friends to get together and fete one person with anything he needs; a two-dollar shower puts an oft-welcome price limit on the budget and fits in anywhere; a perfume shower is self-explanatory; a household shower fills the needs of the guest of honor; a cupboard shower helps put needed items on empty shelves.

How to Make Space Spheres

Inexpensive and always welcome decorations for any shower are the space spheres. Here's how to make them:

1. Mix equal portions of instant laundry starch powder and cold water for papier-mâché paste. Let stand a few minutes to thicken.
2. Soak string, cord, yarn or twine in solution and wrap around and around criss-cross fashion on large blown-up balloons. Scatter on glitter or sequins for celestial brilliance.
3. Hang to dry. Pop balloons and pull away. Suspend spheres from ceiling with strong twine or colored thread.

Suggestion: To make other papier-mâché creations, dip newspaper strips, colored tissue, cotton balls, facial tissues or yarn in the same starch solution and mold over wire or other forms.

How to Make Play Clay

You may want to make your own toys or novelties to suit very individual showers. Here's how to make play clay:

1. Stir 1 cup cornstarch and 2 cups baking soda together in a saucepan. Mix in 1¼ cups cold water and stir constantly over medium heat. Mixture will thin, then thicken.
2. When it reaches a moist "mashed potato" consistency, remove from heat, turn out on a plate and cover with a damp cloth to cool. Knead like dough. Work with a portion at a time, storing the rest in a plastic bag to prevent it from drying.
3. Roll the clay on waxed paper and cut with cooky cutters and knives or mold it into figures appropriate for the shower
4. Dry on paper, turning pieces occasionally.

5. When dry and hard, glue on pin or earring backs for jewelry. Finish with colorful paint designs and coat with clear plastic, shellac or nail polish.

How to Make Color Sunglasses

A mod style calls for wearing the bright pastel colored sunglasses. You can color your own. Here's how:

Dye white or clear vinyl plastic sunglasses in a solution of ½ bottle dye liquid or 1 (1⅛ ounce) package dye powder dissolved in 1 quart hot tap water. Immerse glasses and rotate gently to dye evenly. When desired color is reached, rinse off excess dye. Pastels are most successful colors. *Tip:* Do not use black or navy colors since these do not come out right on sunglasses.

Have Pleasant Party Shower Talk

Of course, if you are having a very informal get-together, conversation could continue around the dinner table, after it has been cleared off. As for watching television, it is best to do this when you are alone. After all, you invite friends because you enjoy their company and their conversation and not to watch television.

How do you keep conversation going? If you are a relaxed hostess, you make your guests feel at ease and conversation will undoubtedly flow without any problems. You need not and should not chatter incessantly. Let talk develop at an easy pace. If anybody has returned from an interesting trip, ask about the journey and start talking that way. *Tip:* An ideal solution is to make certain to invite at least three to five guests who are lively conversationalists.

Clothes: Use Good Taste and Common Sense

Regarding clothes, wear something comfortable. The floor-length hostess dresses are very popular. The long lines are flattering to most women. They allow the freedom to curl up on the floor to chat with a friend if one desires. Wear any light color or elegant fabric you wish.

Suggestion: If you're going to be doing some cooking, avoid ruffles at the wrist which can be a hazard near the oven; avoid slipper satin which can look a disaster if the stew bubbles over.

A considerate hostess will suggest to her guests how they dress. In many communities, a shower party may conjure an image of formal clothes. Actually, an informal wool is more appropriate. Whatever your plans, advise all your guests. A lady feels quite ill at ease if she wears lace decolletage when everyone else is in high-necked suits.

How to Hold Food When Guests Are Late

If you have any idea that some guests might be late, plan a menu with this possibility in mind. Short-order foods to cook on arrival may be broiled chops cooked in minutes, gelatin salad from the refrigerator and a dessert that needs no last-minute processing.

Tip: choose a casserole which can be kept at serving temperature on an electric warming tray or in a warm oven. Choose a dessert that can be popped straight from freezer to table.

Suggestion: Some foods can be salvaged for the latecomer. If the entrée is a roast, wait until guests arrive to carve. A roast will retain some heat for quite a while. Serve gravy sizzling hot and no one will notice the not-so-hot roast.

Many foods can be kept in serving condition in tightly covered containers over hot, not boiling, water.

Vegetables will hold up rather well for 15 minutes or a half hour if kept over hot water. If the delay is very long, add a cream soup to vegetables or drain and then marinate in French dressing.

Wrap rolls in aluminum foil and keep warm on electric warming tray or in the oven.

Spaghetti can wait! Drain in a colander over a pan containing small amount of boiling water. Coat spaghetti with small amount of butter to keep strands from sticking.

Tea sandwiches will stay fresh without curling if you place a clean dampened tea towel or napkin over them and keep in a cool spot.

Keep a fresh pot of coffee brewing and all will be right with the world. Make your late-arriving guests feel welcome and you'll have a successful shower party.

"Until the Next Shower Party . . . "

Now it is the end of the evening and your shower party has been a happy success. No one really wants to go, but leave they must "until the next shower party . . ."

They all say their "Thank-you's," and "goodbyes," but all too frequently one couple stays on and on. How do you get them to leave? After a polite interval, you can gather up ash-trays and used glasses. If they still don't take the hint, you can say that much as you'd love to continue talking, John has to work tomorrow. If it's a Saturday date, he has an early tennis or golf date. Tell them you'll look forward to having them again. The shower party has been wonderful . . . so good night!

16.

How To Be a Shower Success

A social history of man could be written in terms of his celebrations. From the earliest written wedding feasts—which were really times when the groom's family fought off the bride's would-be rescuers—to contemporary outdoor parties, these celebrations have reflected the social sense, the concerns and the joys of the occasion.

In brief, here is how you can be a shower success:

1. Choose guests for an interesting interplay of character and attitudes but avoid personalities that will sharply clash.

2. Set a shower mood and a theme for your party and carry out the theme from invitation to decoration, food and the selection of gifts.

3. Let guests in on your party plan in advance so they'll prepare for it and enjoy it more.

4. Be comfortable with what you have for equipment; make use of disposable ware.

5. Make the most of color, design and unique interest in your table setting and no one will question its cost.

6. Set your table to reflect the warmth of your welcome and the theme of the occasion, rather than cold correctness; it'll make for a happier shower party.

PLACE CARD DESIGNS

Cut from construction paper.
Draw designs with felt tip pens.

Ancient Greek Revival

Gay Nineties

Sportsman's

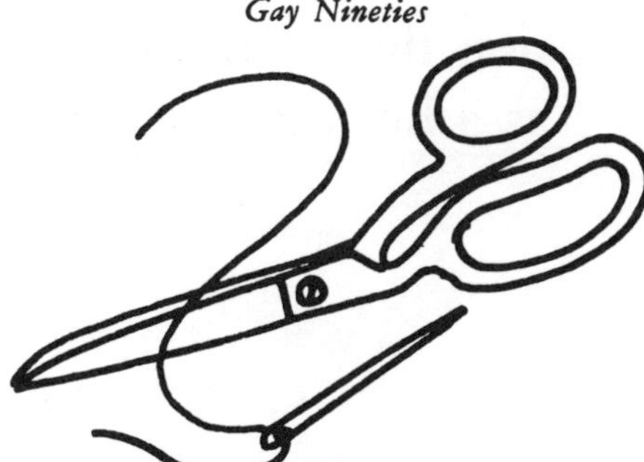

Sewing Notions

Hawaiian

Candlelight

Beach or Pool

Spanish

7. Take advantage of easy serving techniques, including self-help at the buffet table and easy-serving dishes.

8. Plan for ease of cleanup by leaving a bag or container in readiness for rubbish, the sink filled with soapy water in which to soak pans, utensils and dishes as they are cleared away.

9. Place cards may be used any time. If you, the hostess are seating more than eight at one table, you will find them more helpful. Cards may be of almost any material, formal or whimsical but keep the theme of the shower in mind.

10. Enjoy your shower party as a fun-filled occasion for good friends to get together.

* * * * *

You can have fun at a shower party by being a guest at your very own party! With observance of the guidelines in this volume, you should have a memorable occasion that will win you praises and make you much sought after as a hostess, guest and —guest of honor!

Index